Up to the Cottage
Memories of Muskoka
Grant D. Fairley

LYNNETTE,
IN APPRECIATION FOR YOUR
MANY KINDNESSES IN OUR
WORK TOGETHER!

Up to the Cottage

Memories of Muskoka

By

Grant D. Fairley

First Edition

Published By: Silverwoods Publishing - a division of McK Consulting Inc.

Toronto ~ Windsor ~ Chicago

978-1-897202-16-6

Cover design by Cari Fairley of Artist's Tree

Printed in Canada

Up to the Cottage

Memories of Muskoka

Grant D. Fairley

Contents

Dedication

This book is dedicated to James Alexander Cowan – Grandpa Cowan – who had the foresight to invest in a place in 1950 that would come to be enjoyed by the four generations who followed. It is also in honour of the many family, friends and neighbours who are part of our cottage story.

Acknowledgements

I would like to begin by acknowledging the patience and encouragement of my wife, Cari as I have taken the time to take our stories and create this book. She loved the cottage as I did and that made us both be willing to face the crazy traffic, packing and unpacking, cleaning and cleaning again that is part of living in Toronto, Ontario and heading north to Muskoka. Credit too to my children for their flexibility with their Dad's strange assortment of projects like this.

My father and mother, Harry and Lois Fairley made decision and sacrifice to purchase the cottage after the death of my grandfather. That investment gave my children and many other people the opportunity to enjoy time at Mary Lake.

Dad took many photographs of cottage life over the years as did we. Those pictures supplemented by others have made this process easier as the pictures trigger many memories in greater detail than might otherwise occur. Thanks to the children here who patiently digitized the old slides and photographs to assist in the book's production and for the website. Great work!

Some of the family members have been kind enough to fill in some of the facts for me. Special thanks to the other relations including Aunts Joan Meuser and Frances Cowan; Uncle Doug Cowan, Aunt Caylee Bailey; and cousins Murray Fitzpatrick, Patty Meuser, Greg and Nancy De Souza. Former cottage neighbour Marion Havercroft was also kind in her assistance on several points. I especially benefitted from the Cowan Family Tree book assembled over the years by Uncle Stuart Cowan and the family. Another important resource came from Jim and Karen Diamond, cousins who did extensive work on the Wood family tree.

One of the extended family, Mary Jolliffe, C.M. the publicist for many years at the Stratford Festival and the Canada Council was generous with her time and recollections about Grandpa Cowan.

Public Relations specialist, Kevin Putnam, as a student and then in preparation for a book did a study on the life of my grandfather James A. Cowan and his role in the history of Public Relations in Canada. My conversations with him have been helpful.

Lindsay Thompson of Marketing Magazine was helpful in securing a 1961 profile of James A. Cowan.

Jessica Allen, the editorial assistant at Maclean's Magazine identified the many articles written by James A. Cowan for Maclean's between the 1920s and the 1940s.

Ken Veitch is someone who loves the history of Bracebridge and the surrounding area. He was useful in my research as well.

Kirsten Maxwell at the Town of Huntsville office was helpful in confirming some of the topographical facts about the lake to aid my fading memory!

Cari's creative artistic talents are responsible for designing the book cover.

Thanks go to Jenny-Lee Boyle for her thoughtful review of this book and comments on its development.

The thorough work of Wendy Carter in editing this book is a credit to not only her skills but also to her patience. Gary Carter and the Kainos team have once again gone above and beyond in setting and formatting the cover and the text within the book with the additional challenge of all the pictures included.

Many other friends and family have taken the time to read drafts of the book and have shared their helpful comments. Thank you!

1. Introduction

Once upon a time, there were simple cottages dotting the northern lakes of Ontario. With their screen doors, latches and screened porches they were early experiments of city dwellers connecting with a still wild country that could be both enchanting and dangerous.

Cottages were not quite convenient in the 1940s, 1950s and 1960s in Muskoka. You had to endure challenging roads, unpredictable services and a "less is more" philosophy of life. These were not the grand resorts or hotels of the time. Cottages then were not houses transplanted from the city. They were often wood and small. Their location meant it was easier to read a book than find a television signal. If you were warm – it was because you knew how to build a fire or wore sweaters – or both.

But cottage life connected families with nature and with each other as a center of activity, rest and reflection. It was a place where you could count on a good night's sleep as much from the "Northern air" as from the many land and lake activities enjoyed there.

This book is a collection of my memories about life at our cottage on Mary Lake, Muskoka, Ontario. The cottage was part of my life from when I was a newborn in 1958 until its sale in 2004. Now with some years passed since it was a hub of our lives, it seemed like a good time to do some remembering on paper (and in cyberspace).

In doing so, I hope I am honouring my grandfather James A. Cowan who originally bought the land and built the cottage. This book recognizes all the family members named and unnamed who were part of its story. We enjoyed the many friends who came to visit and shared cottage life with us. Our thanks go to the original and later neighbours who added their friendship and textures to the adventures there. Finally, to all the people of Port Sydney, Utterson, Huntsville, Bracebridge, Gravenhurst, Algonquin and Dorset who tolerated another of the cottage families, we are glad you were there too.

For the many people in Ontario who had "cottage" as part of their story, I hope that this book will remind you of the experiences you had in Muskoka, the Kawarthas, The Lake of Bays or elsewhere. I have enjoyed visiting cottages and cabins in many different places like New Hampshire, Vermont, the Adirondacks, Michigan, Wisconsin, Minnesota, Mississippi, North Carolina, Arizona and California. While they all are distinctive with the regional difference, they share some common cottage themes. For those who enjoyed cottage (or cabin) life in other parts of Canada, the U.S., or else-where, I trust that you will find part of your story here in the shared experiences that all cottagers understand so well.

This is not a "researched" book. The memories included here are largely my own and so feature the impressions I experienced. If there are factual errors – I hope that they can be forgiven as part of the nature of reminiscing.

Our cottage of old lives on in our memories, our photographs, videos and stories. Now it is also in this book.

The cottage has passed beyond us but after reading this, I hope you will feel like you have been there too.

2. Into the Mist

One of the most magical times at the cottage was the early morning canoe ride. Later in the summer as the lake was warm and the morning air was cooler, you could enjoy a paddle into another world as the sea smoke enveloped your canoe.

With a flat and calm lake, these mornings would be a time for total relaxation as the only sounds would be the occasional call of the loon or the voice of the train in the distance as it made its way through forest and rock. Each stroke of the paddle took you further into the mist where you might only see a few feet ahead in any direction. Then you could let yourself drift in that peaceful calm. It was as close to a natural connection between a person and nature you could make on the lake. No sounds created. No wake was washing across the lake to disturb those creatures far or near. There you were a part of the beauty around you and yet hidden by that same nature that created such a beautiful hour.

We had a large red, fiberglass canoe with a square back at the stern.

Most of our canoe trips were spent going parallel to the shoreline as the waves of Mary Lake could be quite impressive and sudden storms were always a concern if you were too far away.

On a calm day, we could move very quickly. The water was clear enough that you could easily look down over the side and see the orange-red sand passing beneath you. The rippled bottom spoke of waves as old as the lake itself. It was like a panorama to see the birch and pine trees and rocks stream by on the shore as the canoe glided through the water. At times, you felt that some baritone announcer on a nature show should be speaking in the background describing the beautiful experience you were enjoying at that time.

On a wavy day, you had to earn the views you would enjoy. We would head into the waves as much as possible with the extra energy required, comforted by the knowledge that the same waves would bring us home with little effort beyond steering the canoe.

One of the favourite destinations was to go south past the Jackson/ Bradley cottage on the point not too far away. There we would turn into the channel that led to the Jackson River. The many grassy sides and small brush that were on the shores of the mouth of the river gave way to a variety of trees that had staked their claim on the water's edge. Turning sharply, we would follow the meandering channel as it split into a couple directions. Always quiet at this point, we would keep a sharp eye for the Great Blue Heron often fishing in the trees or in the shallow streams there. If we saw any of the many leopard frogs or the occasional over-sized bullfrog, we were careful to suggest that they sing another day when the heron was not around. We also might encounter a beaver making its way with some soft poplar or other sticks en route to the beaver lodge further up the river.

When the breeze was gone and the air still, the warmth of the day would be captured in the grasses and reflections off the water. Some water striders would provide us with an escort as we paddled along. Bubbles coming from the decaying bottom (or beavers holding their breath!) always made you imagine the unknowns of the bottom of the tea coloured water in that river. Further up, we would have to dodge the ever-changing maze of fallen logs with the familiar sound of us sliding over top of one of the submerged victims of beaver teeth, changing shores or age.

If the water level was high enough, we could make it all the way to the foaming bottom of the Jackson Falls. Peering up the water covered cliffs we could enjoy the sounds of that water cascading down the rocks and rushing over the rapids at the bottom with the many stones left there over the eons.

Sometimes we would stop for a picnic lunch. Other times we would turn the canoe and follow the river back out to the lake we loved so much.

The canoe was meant for Muskoka and Muskoka for the canoe. Many hours were spent exploring the shorelines and the islands of the lake. Each trip was unique as the ever-changing sky, water and wind would reward you for picking up the paddles once again.

3. The Cottage

There was a screen door. It had a simple latch you would open by pressing down your thumb. You would hear a gentle tap as the spring closed the door after you. You had just passed through into that special place we knew as the cottage.

The old screen door like the old wooden cottages that dotted the lakes of old Muskoka are now hard to find outside of memory. In their place are the bricks and mortar buildings larger than many houses in the cities of Ontario. These new buildings feature designs and use of space that are worthy of being in an architect's magazine. Their size and conveniences make them a contrast to their forerunners on the lake. Are these grand homes a cottage? That may be a point of debate. But there was a time when a cottage was a cottage was a cottage.

The bright white wooden cottage with the blue trim that we enjoyed was built in the late 1950s on Mary Lake, Muskoka. Constructed on the eastern shore of the lake, it was on a cliff overlooking some trees and the waterfront below. The view from the porch included islands and the shore across the lake.

It was a three-bedroom layout with a small restroom, a family room with many windows facing south and a kitchen on the north side. At the lake end of the building was a screened in porch overlooking the lake.

A series of windows separated the main room from the screened porch that was the width of the cottage. On the screened porch were a couple of wooden chairs, an old barrel and a small metal picnic table. The screened porch also featured a classic screen door and latch exiting on to a small porch with wooden stairs extending down in both directions.

The woods around the cottage included a wide range of hardwoods like maple and oak. Silver birch trees and some evergreens were on the cliff heading down to the lake. The soil around the cottage was soft brown sand with wild strawberries growing on the north side.

The size of the cottage was about 1000 square feet.

Nothing special about this building or this place.

Except for everything that happened there over the next 50 years.

4. Go North Young Man – Somehow

S o it would begin.

The car would be packed. The trunk would be crammed with all the real and imagined necessities for the weekend or the week. The "snail" top was added to the roof. The snail was filled. The forgotten playpen was stuffed in some space that we did not know could be there. The car – now a beast of burden – was ready to make the trek north.

One of our children was reliably carsick which meant at any time we could have the added trauma of strange sounds followed by bad smells to make a long journey perfect.

Each mile north of the 401 seemed like a major achievement on a Friday night. By the time we saw the valley of Holland Landing, there seemed to be hope. Stopping in Gasoline Alley north of Barrie was usually required for the children if not the gas tank. Orillia! Now we are cracking the back of the journey.

Then it was the chance to resist or give in to temptation. Resistance was usually futile if the OPEN sign was still lit. Weber's was one of the rewards for enduring the ordeal. The memorable hamburgers, fries and shakes could be enjoyed on the road, out of doors on one of the many picnic tables, or in the wonderful old railway passenger cars.

Another landmark of the northern journey would be the Sundial Restaurant and motel built in the 1960s with its unique sundial on the restaurant and its beautiful view.

We always felt like we had crossed the magical boundary to Muskoka when we could see the outcropping of Canadian Shield rocks as we crossed the bridge at Port Severn. It was official when you spied the sign welcoming us to Muskoka. We would wave to those travelers veering off along the Severn River or Sparrow Lake. Then we would junction to the North while 169 entered Gravenhurst and carried them along to the many smaller and larger lakes en route to Bala. Once you passed that point, you were soooo close. Just the Muskoka Airport and Bracebridge to get by. Then it was just High Falls and Stephenson Roads to see.

The strategy for the children became one of naming the cities and towns we would pass before we would see the signs for Mary Lake and Port Sydney. At times we felt like an unpaid conductor on the CN and later Via Rail or Ontario Northern trains calling out, "Orillia will be next – – – Orillia!" We knew we had achieved something special when the children began to recite the place names for the journey and we could retire as conductors.

Depending on the decade, our entry point for Port Sydney and Mary Lake may have been Muskoka Road 10 that entered Port from the north. In later years, the improved the South Mary Lake Road was the one we would take.

The northern route took you by one of the community cemeteries and then as you went over a hill the first glimpse of Mary Lake and its islands would appear. Regardless of your age or stage, you celebrated that sighting with equal parts of joy and relief. Rounding the bend into the village, a sunny day would reveal the dark blue Mary Lake with some motorboats and sailboats crisscrossing the beautiful water.

South Mary Lake Road would take you past Smitty's gas station and restaurant. Continuing down the very straight but often bumpy road, you would go by a tall stand of old pines that seemed to be standing at attention for our arrival. Then you link up with Muskoka Road 10 coming from the village and cross the bridge that crosses the south branch of the Muskoka River. If your windows were down, you could hear the rapids to your left and see the water flowing to the south along the Muskoka River.

Proceeding around the east side of the lake, we would pass many familiar landmarks that would announce that the cottage was close. We always watched for the sign for the Cliff House Lodge and then the Muskoka Lodge located near the Jackson property.

Up and down a couple of more hills and you would see a small cut in the brush with the sign COWAN waiting to greet you.

We were there!

5. A Greater Purpose

It is said among people of faith that if you survive near death experiences that there must be a greater purpose left in your life or that God is not finished with you yet – or perhaps God is not ready for you!

Those who survived life on the early back roads of Muskoka were people who regularly defied death and experienced the rush of adrenalin that comes with sheer terror.

Muskoka Road 10 in its earlier incarnations was such a road. As was true with many of the original roads connecting the towns and villages of Muskoka, the engineering was focused on getting from A to B with little thought to the blind spots, grading and slopes of the road. The roads were equivalent to a lane and a half that had in many places wild turns and sharp corners. The roads also included enough ups and downs that they might qualify as roller coasters today.

In many places, the roads were sufficiently dangerous that you had to honk your horn as you were approaching some of the most difficult turns and hills to improve the odds that you would not be colliding with another nerve wracked driver heading the other way. Another trick at night was to watch the hydro wires in the distance for the reflection of lights that signaled an approaching car.

On the back road of Mary Lake on Muskoka Road 10 was an old stone bridge not far from the cottage entrance that narrowed to a single lane at the bottom of the hill. This old stone bridge is still visible on the west side of the road and crosses the stream that eventually turns into the Jackson Falls.

If you were able to get past that bridge without incident and over the next hill, you could quickly dash off Muskoka 10 and head down our pleasantly isolated cottage road.

6. The Road More Traveled

The cottage road as we were growing up was known as Cowan Lane (or also as Langbank Lane connecting the cottage to some of the Cowan family history in Dawn Township in Lambton County.) The three-quarters of a mile of Cowan Lane connected Muskoka Road 10 and the cottage.

Like most of the original cottage roads, the term "road" was very generous. In fact, it might be better described as a path where a lane used to exist. The two paths did seem to run on a parallel course but between them grew a mound of grass that crowned several inches higher than the trails.

Depending on the amount of rainfall, the cottage road would have many puddles, ruts and holes to test the suspension and integrity of your car. The high center mound served as a muffler massager at best and a gift to the car repair station at worst. Thankfully, in the good old days the kinds of cars that traversed the cottage road were substantial and solid giving them a fair chance of making it to the cottage in one piece.

The road, like the cottage, represented a combination of delight and labour. One of the regular chores of cottage life with the old road was the clearing of debris and stones that would find their way on the path. After storms, this could be small and large branches and even trees. The healthy rain and sunshine always combined to create the need to scythe the road with this long metal tool that stood as large as we did. You would learn the scything action of taking the blade back and forth while holding the top and middle handles. It was very effective against all manner of growth in the middle-of-the-road and along the edges. However, it was a lot of work. When you are too young to hold the large scythe but old enough to be responsible you had the job of using the sickle to fell whatever could be reached.

A walk down the road would take you through a variety of environments. Closest to the cottage were the stands of oaks and birches. Further on the trail to an opening known as the "golf course" (part of the old Edgemere Golf Course c. WWII) there were meadows with their long grasses. Through the dark forest made up of many different hardwoods and fir trees was the most threatening part of the journey for the timid explorer. Then opening to the large meadow to the south forest dotted with some coniferous and deciduous trees that had established themselves. To the north were the poplars and ferns leading once more into a forested area. In the early years the trail passed Uncle Doug's* Gate that was neatly constructed with a tie rope to close the cottage road in the off-season. As you neared the end of the road, you walked parallel to the stream that sometimes could be heard falling over the moss covered rocks after a good rainfall.

A jog to the north put you at Muskoka Road 10 where for many years was posted a sign that seemed very official and important when we were children. It was there before the age of bilingualism and biculturalism. It read in large letters "Défense de Cracher!" As children, we assumed this meant not to have a car crash. Only later did we learn that it was part of my grandfather's sense of humour that announced "No Spitting Allowed."

*Uncle Doug Cowan is the younger brother of my mother. He served in the Ministry of Transportation in the Public Relations area. He is best known for his work on the Driver's Handbook that we all studied to get our licence in Ontario. When driving ahead from his great-uncle, my oldest son received the compliment that he had avoided the typical young driver "jack-rabbit starts" after stopping. This was high praise from the Driving Jedi Master!

7. What's That Smell?

Cottages like most buildings have their own distinctive smell. Particularly those cottages that are seasonal tend to have certain scents that change with the calendar and the activities of the cottage dwellers. If you are coming from the city to Muskoka, you already experienced the freshening of the air and the richness of the oxygen as you made your way past civilization. Along South Mary Lake Road, we would drive by a series of white pines standing guard that exuded a wonderful pine scent that confirmed we were getting close to the beloved cottage. Stepping out of the car at the cottage, our senses were greeted by a variety of smells from the leaf litter in the forest to the breeze from the lake depending on the time of day and the weather. It was quite a contrast from discerning the metallic smells of industrial Windsor or the smell of grains being processed at Hiram Walker's downtown. Those first few moments at the cottage offered a bouquet of distinctive reminders that you were in Muskoka.

When it came time to open the screen door and then unlock the main door, it was as if the cottage exhaled the breath that it had held since the cottage was closed in the fall. You could take in the combination of wood and fabrics that had been waiting to be reawakened for the summer season. As is traditional for most cottage goers, this important event typically was connected to May 24th weekends. The new flowers might be planted and some potted plants were spread around the property to add some extra colour during those first couple of months there. It was that wonderful time of hope and optimism for a new cottage season.

The best mornings – even if the floors were cold – were when you awoke to the smell of bacon and eggs cooking and coffee percolating. Mom would often also have a batch of Quaker Oats bubbling which she assured us would "Stick to your ribs." When questioned why we would want oatmeal or anything else stuck to our ribs – she explained that this would keep us from getting hungry rather than eating something that was digested quickly. We felt better about the oatmeal after that. Adding to that the wisps of smoke coming from the fireplace and traveling up the chimney to be carried away through the woods, you had a perfect Muskoka morning.

The only thing that could surpass the ecstasy of that experience in cottage life would be to catch the hint of smoke as you returned from an early-morning canoe ride in the mists of Mary Lake and find those smoky scents also included the bacon and eggs and coffee as you opened the door. Of course, the aroma of Grandma's meals or baking would also enchant any-one who experienced it.

Growing up in the 1960s when smoking was more prevalent meant that you could become quite a connoisseur of tobacco smells as a boy even if you did not smoke. (Thankfully, it was not something our family ever did. We had other vices of course...see paragraphs above...) Grandpa Cowan used to smoke cigarettes and then on a whim switched to cigars. We became used to smelling the scent of some very fine cigars as we would walk on the road or sit on the screened porch. His favourite brand (based on the beauti-ful wooden boxes we received for storing little boy stuff like marbles) was White Owl.

As mentioned elsewhere, the first Gandalf I knew was the kind grandfatherly Ben Jackson from the original cottage who was very senior in years when I remember meeting him. He was one of those talented pipe smokers who could blow smoke rings, allow wisps to float up or just puff gently on the sweet smelling tobacco. Did I mention he could blow smoke out his ears? Remarkable sights for a young boy to see.

There were many smells of the cottage as you roamed through the woods, in the ferns, over the meadows, in the dark forest, by the beaver dam, under the pines, on the beach and in the lake. Each one of these aromas is imprinted on memories and emotions of those growing up at the cottage in Muskoka.

8. Warm Thoughts

Like most of the old cottages in Muskoka, the buildings were not winterized and were poorly insulated if there was any insulation at all. That meant that all of the heating would come from the wood stoves or fireplaces. These stoves and fireplaces were based on very inefficient designs. That was part of their charm, for you could count on these old fireplaces to allow just enough smoke to escape to make the air fragrant and cozy. Our first fireplace was an old acorn style design. It had chain mesh that closed the opening and later an additional cover flat. It was located in the main room near the kitchen and in spite of its small size was able to generate wonderful heat and many happy memories entertaining young and old alike with its dancing flames and glowing embers.

It was a great honour to be selected as one of the fire starters in the cottage. Apart from the creation of wonderful cottage meals, no role was as important as keeping everyone warm at night or in the morning with a great fire. So the fire starter had to know the art and craft of balancing paper, kindling, softwood and later hardwood so that the fire would grow warm enough to reach the corners of the cottage without becoming so hot that you had the dreaded chimney fire. Once the ingredients were loaded on the small grill inside the fireplace it was time to bring out the wooden matches.

At our cottage, it was always tradition to have one or more boxes of Eddy's matches. The wooden matches were always secured in an old white oatcakes tin famously marked "Matches". As we learned at an early age, matches must always be kept in secure metal tins because of the risk of mice entering the cottage, chewing the matches and starting a bonfire.

Ideally, you have with the matches one of the strike pads that allow you to zip the wooden match along its rough surface until ignition happens. However, from time to time, there were no such strips available or they had been worn down to the point that they had no friction. That would lead you to a variety of less reliable solutions ranging from using the side of the fireplace (a definite no-no with my mother), a nearby stone or other rough surface.

Some of the more ingenious methods used by the teenagers could include striking one match head against the other, using the flick of a finger-nail or the classic zipper strike where one risked much more than he knew in order to light that match. One visitor even lit a match using their front tooth but I digress...

It is said that much can be told about the cottage owners by the various fireplace tools available for use. In our case, traditionally there were a couple of poker options including the long straight poker with the hook on the end and the heavier iron poker that could grab and lift logs with its horse-shoe shape. We also had a very old pair of asbestos gloves that taught us our first lessons about the importance of insulation against heat. Various brushes to tidy the hearth area could be found standing near the most controversial of the fireplace items – the bellows. We must confess that in later years we too succumbed to the temptation of having bellows to concentrate the air on the slowly burning logs. In the earliest days however, it was blood, sweat and breath that was required to ensure that the fire not only began well but also kept going.

In the early days, the fireplace was used to minimize the amount of garbage that would be taken to the dump. This was a favorite duty of the age-appropriate children who would take the cereal boxes, tissues and other paper goods to put into the fireplace. Back in the days when our milk was provided in wax cartons, we were always pleased when someone finished the milk. That meant that the wax carton could be put on the fire and we would get to enjoy listening to the crackles and whispers as the old carton would burn. Occasionally it would even show some colors.

It was also a bonus if you had the foresight to collect some pine-cones along with the kindling. Throwing a few pinecones onto the burning fire would add some snap, crackle and pop. We also learned that wood that was not seasoned could sizzle and pop as the sap still in the wood boiled and expanded. Little wonder that the fireplace became a center of attention as it provided a variety of sights and smells to entertain both young and old.

One of the rewards of having the fireplace was the roasting of marsh-mallows. In the early days, this meant finding the appropriate sticks or hang-ers to foist the marshmallows over the glowing embers. While you would assume that roasting marshmallows is a learnable skill, we had friends and family who could find a way to flame any marshmallow no matter how gentle the embers were glowing. Coincidentally, these people tended to be the most generous in sharing their burnt offerings with others. Those marshmallow specialists who were able to consistently provide a lightly browned marsh-mallow warmed gently and ready to fall off the stick were especially valued members of the tribe. Rare and wonderful those perfect marshmallows!

Many years later, we replaced the dear old fireplace with an airtight wood-burning stove. Bringing in the new stove through the narrow cottage door involved an engineering feat akin to getting a ship in the bottle, as my brother the then future engineer, was able to twist and turn this monstros-ity through the small space. I saw it happen and I still do not believe it. The new wood-burning stove required some different skills as you had to master the setting of the newly sized fire and then open the circular vents to just the right setting to allow the air to go rushing by the wood. With some experi-ence, it was possible to turn the art of the fireplace into the science of the wood-burning stove. With a much larger capacity, the new woodstove was able to heat the cottage faster and warmed even the most distant corners of the bedrooms.

It took many years of experience to know exactly what size log was needed to maintain or build heat for the cottage family. Then of course as the evening drew to a close, there was the important selection of hardwoods that would burn slowly to keep the chill off the cottage overnight. It was always a sign of great virtue if you were the one who first thing in the morning before anyone else had stirred made your way over to the fireplace and fed the fire so that the others would wake up a little warmer. It seemed to be a fact of cottage life that no matter when the morning fire began, the cottage floor was able to maintain its chill sufficiently to awaken you instantly once those feet touched the tiles. Even now, burning wood in the air reminds us of cottage life.

9. Cottage Worthy

In the days before designer cottages included designer furniture and accents, cottages would be the accumulation of strange and diverse pieces of furniture, wall hangings and knickknacks. Often these were items from the family home that had been replaced and now were at the cottage. Coming as we did from Scottish roots, it was always amazing to see how many items could be deemed "cottage worthy" even though they had "dump worthy" featured on them. In our case, there was a complication of bringing something all the way from Windsor through Toronto and up to the cottage. Over the course of the 6+ hours of traveling there was always a risk of weather conditions that could make a bad couch worse. So mom always enjoyed hunting locally for those people who were discarding some of their furniture to find a piece that could work at the cottage. One of the realities of cottage life that we all understood was that not only did the furniture not match but that no amount of squinting could reconcile the shades, patterns, and styles of the furniture. To compensate for the lack of coordination, each piece of furniture became an unofficial artifact with the accompanying stories that would recount how it was found and what adventures were experienced in its transport to the cottage. Each strange piece of furniture then went from being unwanted to being celebrated for its uniqueness.

In the case of a shared family cottage, you also had the variety of tastes and interests that each part of the family brought to the decorating. To be sure, one always tried to allow for an overall theme set by the matriarch of the day but inevitably through gifts and remembrances accumulated over many visits all sorts of new pieces and motifs would appear. Thankfully, my mother was not so vain as to hide some of the more unsightly items until their donors visited again. But it was always interesting to see what pieces were relegated to what rooms in the cottage.

Of course, many special items formed part of the childhood memories of being at the cottage. These often included items that were one of a kind and could not be found elsewhere. We used this strategy quite intentionally with our children by having toys that were available to cottage and not available at home. Like old friends, these toys would await them at the cottage and became that much more special because of the emotional connections made there.

In the earliest days of the cottage, the gyprock walls were very plain. One of my cousins, Patty, who has always been artistic used the shape of the hanging iron poker and drew around it to give it a suitable face and body. Unlike a straight poker, this one had an oval at the top to hold and then at the bottom it was designed to lift logs with what looked like legs. Somehow putting the poker back where it belonged was easier than many other jobs because of the smiling face on the wall that awaited the return of its body.

A couple of wooden characters that I particularly enjoyed were known as Salty and Peppy. Each was a simply painted wooden salt and pepper shaker. They had enchanting faces with coats of primary colors. Their necks would extend up and down as you shook out the salt or pepper. Sometimes they would make a squeaking sound. Salty and Peppy lived at the cottage and therefore only shared our summers. It was always special to open the cottage door and find them sitting on the shelf in the kitchen waiting for us as much as we were waiting for them.

Hot cocoa was also a mainstay of cottage life. On particularly cold mornings or dreary days it was great to have a cup of cocoa with some miniature marshmallows floating on top. While cocoa may be served successfully in a variety of mugs and cups, our cocoa was always served in special old glazed brown cocoa mugs. Like so many of the important cottage traditions, they began somewhere quite innocently and then at some point became something special to be celebrated.

One of the early appliances that we used at the cottage was an old-fashioned toaster. You may have seen these in museums or antique stores but we actually grew up using them. These toasters had a door on each side of the device and you would lay your bread on the open door. In closing the door, the toast would be brought close to the heating element in the center of the toaster. Unlike our toasters of today which measure the heat and toast both sides at once, these toasters required you to pay close attention to how the toast was doing. When the toast had reached the appropriate level of toasting, you would open the door (and if your wrist action was sufficiently skilled) the piece of bread would flip to the untoasted side. You would then close the door and repeat the process. Once your toast was done he would unplug the toaster and enjoy your toast. Because it was so different from the toasters at home, this and other ancient monstrosities became highly valued as part of cottage memories.

Very few things were electrified at the cottage. There were a few inside lights but no tradition of ceiling lights beyond the lamps spread throughout the cottage. Dad had successfully transformed a couple of large pieces of driftwood that were found on the beach into some driftwood lamps. These lamps were not only unique but a great place for little boys to hide marbles and army men in the many nooks and crannies.

Of course, we did not have a doorbell. Even if one might have been constructed and installed, it would not have suited the cottage. Instead, those visiting the cottage could announce their arrival by using the woodpecker. The woodpecker with the appropriate combination of black white and red was stationed on the left side of the main door. It was attached to a slice of birch bark log with the metal chain hanging down from it. By pulling, the chain created a distinctive knocking sound that would tell one and all that you had arrived in a way that suited cottage life. Along with the simple latch and the screen door, you felt welcomed to a simpler time and place where the focus was not on wealth but on a gentle approach to life.

As the generations aged and we began to experience our own set of aches and pains, we were now sympathetic to those pieces of furniture that were happy to be deemed at least cottage worthy.

10. Sounds of Silence

The old cottages were especially suited for giving people a sense of being together. Part of this was the size of the building; part of this was the walls – or what passed for walls. These were often just sheets of gyprock or some thin paneling attached to the studs that separated the rooms. The tops of these walls were often left open to allow the air to circulate.

All this meant that there was little that could go on in the cottage that could not be heard by anyone who did not have his or her hearing aid out. And even then…

This meant that if there were any disputes or uncomfortable moments for a couple, you had best take a walk down the road. It also helped to be down wind as well so your voices would not carry. Otherwise, everyone in the cottage would know whatever it was that you were discussing no matter how well you practiced the art of whispering. Some family members prided themselves on their expert hearing and if the whispers did grow too faint, they would call out to have the volume raised ever so slightly so they would not miss the good parts.

The use of the solo restroom would also leave little to the imagination. Some tried to cover the inevitable sounds by running water or humming a tune. (Although some tunes seemed to have a strong percussion part played at the strangest moments!) Of course, there were others who let nature take its course with full fury.

Nighttime could provide its own humour or challenges. It seemed to be worse if only one of the cottagers snored. If two snored, you may have an antiphonal resonance. If more than two snored, you relied on the adage that if people can get used to sleeping near the "L" trains in Chicago – it was possible to sleep in Muskoka. Now I have never met someone who actually lived and slept near the elevated trains in the Windy City so perhaps that is as much an urban myth as being one of the few non-snoring types in a cottage full of noisy snoozers.

Not all the night sounds were troubling. A gentle breeze might rustle the leaves. Raindrops falling on the cottage roof provided a sleepy ambiance for anyone there. The call of the loons or the far off gulls was peaceful. Perhaps my favourite was the sound of a distant train making its way through the woods and by the rock faces; that is the Muskoka we love.

11. On the Surface

The lakes of Muskoka offer many ways to enjoy your time no matter what your age or stage of life. For us it was the full range of experiences in motorboats with their high powered engines, fishing boats with their modest power, row boats with the brute force required, canoes with their human energy, sailboats that used the wind and kayaks that used your imagination. There were also the rafts and docks that connected you to a variety of activities on the water.

For those who have never seen it, Mary Lake is about 4 miles (6500m) from one end to the other with the shore across from us about 1.25 miles (2000m) in distance. For us a trip to Port Sydney was about 1.8 miles (3000m) to get there. The lake has a maximum depth of 183 feet in the trench carved long ago by the glaciers of the ice age that covered the area. It has about 16 miles of shoreline with assorted islands. Its largest island is Crown that is aptly named as it looks like a crown. It has a beautiful boathouse and cottage with an especially enchanting small bridge and walkway on the north side of the island. We were about equidistant to Snowshoe toward Port Sydney and Cox (better known to us as Dead Man's) Island to the northwest. Both of those nearby islands were great for fishing. Snowshoe has a wonderfully designed cottage with a great view. Dead Man's is owned by Camp Mini-Yo-We and is used for overnight camping. The other islands include Rock, Gall, Bonner, Rumbles and Forest.

One of the facts I really enjoyed was that the water clarity (a measurement of how far you can see and therefore how free the water is of particles that absorb and scatter the light measured with a Secchi disk – learned something new!) was over 11 feet (3.4m). We would love to canoe out into the water to watch what a long way we could go and still see the bottom.

Our red sand beach was limited in the early years and most of the time was spent at what we would later call "the second beach", located to the north of where the stairs came down. The beach usually had assorted beach toys (no matter what the age of the kids, we always enjoyed building sand castles) along with some folding wooden chairs with blue and white canvas attached. It was all very simple – and simply magnificent.

With those boats came the opportunities to water ski (Dad could still ski and even slalom in his early 50s!) and bounce around on tubes or boards being pulled behind the boat. One of the local camps had a banana boat. It was great fun to watch this yellow streak go bouncing by on the waves with campers holding on for dear life and the thrill of the ride.

The sailboats were beautiful to watch. It was more of a challenge to use my brother's Sea Snark. It was a one-person sailboat. You were supposed to lift your sail, control your draft, steer the rudder and tack with the wind. This was all to be done – preferably – with the boat still upright. Many the novice cottage sailor was glad for shallows and sandbars as they tried to right the sailboat after a good wind or bad balance tipped her over.

The original rowboat was wooden that had arrived on the ice one spring. Unclaimed from the note posted at Clark's General Store, it stayed with us. The boat was quite old and decayed but it did allow us to have a first taste of boating as little boys. As with many things in those early days, the lake giveth and the lake taketh away so it continued its journey elsewhere after a summer.

Over the years, we progressed to a 14-foot aluminum boat great for fishing – except you had to row to get anywhere – not so bad when the lake was calm but a challenge when the winds of Mary created some wonder-ful swells. But we were young and full of energy – or at least the power to negotiate so the rowing was shared. Later that boat had a smaller motor and finally a 9.5 hp Mercury. We were never so glad to see nine horses as we were when it joined the family. That got us all over the lake – if not fast then safely. It was small enough that it gave the younger children the experience of having their hand on the throttle while the parent beside guided their time.

The motor boat meant visiting the marina – the only marina on Mary

Lake. Al Smith owned and operated it for many years. In addition to filling the large gas can with its primer ball and black hose that sat at the back of the boat, he would entertain with news of the lake. There were always volunteers for this task as a visit to the marina usually meant a cold pop or an ice cream bar – my dad's favourite.

At various times we enjoyed friends bringing up faster boats and from time to time we went waterskiing or tubing on Mary Lake or elsewhere. But it was our old faithful motor boat that was always there to take us on the lake to enjoy the sun, to explore the shoreline with its many ever changing cottages or to just feel that breeze on your face as you moved against the wind and waves. You could usually spot our white Muskoka chairs in the distance with the hints of red sand waiting for you.

We often took the dog(s) out with us. All of them were water dogs who enjoyed swimming. At the point we were heading toward the cottage and about the location where clam land would be, we would let the dogs jump into the lake for their swim to the shore. In addition to the exercise, they enjoyed the cool swim after being in the sun. They would give the boat a good race into shore as the children would cheer them on.

In the evening, it was a treat to be anchored off of Dead Man's Island and listen to the campfire songs at Mini-Yo-We as they gathered together at the point under the tall pines.

Mary Lake was a place to learn the protocols of waving to each passing boat along with the people on shore. These waves were the up stretched hand – not usually full of motion. You either did not force a response from the intended recipient of the wave or embarrass yourself if perchance they did not notice you and you continued to wave in a way that appeared needy.

You also had to learn the appropriate speed and distance so that your boat did not cause problems for lesser sailboats, canoes or kayaks who really did not want to be swamped by your rush past them. Once you had been on the receiving end of a big wave when you were in a canoe, you understood how important a little consideration was to keeping everyone safe.

It was great to pass by an odd classic wooden Peterborough boat that would venture on the lake. Dave Wagner for a time had a houseboat that could be seen going up and down the lake. A tour boat was used by Muskoka Bible Conference for a while. It was a strange feeling to be part of someone's tour while we were swimming or relaxing on the beach. The many colourful sailboats always made it a pleasant picture with the deep blues of the lake and the bright blue of the sun. Later on, it would be windsurfers who could be seen crisscrossing the waters. The water was a place we enjoyed being whether it was under it, in it or on the surface.

As the day was dying and the darkness was starting to envelope our lake, we would start the engine and head back toward the cottage. It did not take long for the light to recede and for the black night to conquer the day. As we were approaching our destination on a cool night, we would focus on that cottage light on the back porch beckoning us home for the warmth of a fire, some hot cocoa and perhaps some cinnamon toast to end our day together.

12. All Creatures Great and Small

Encountering creatures (the non-human kind) at the cottage was a part of wilderness life in the earlier days. It still happened later on, but not as frequently as there were more people and more traffic.

We could expect to see some of the more courageous (or foolhardy?) animals like the chipmunks most days at the cottage. They would scamper around between the open areas and the woods, never far from the safety of a bush or patch of brush. They were quite happy to share any of the birdseed you might have left out in the feeders. Squirrels too would happen by and also claim a perch on the feeder until full cheeks meant full tummy.

The beach also spoke of other visitors during the night. Most often, it was the distinctive feet of the raccoon that left their mark. Those "masked bandits" could be entertaining or a nuisance. If you were sleeping in the tent outside, they were alarming with the chattering and moving around. But they could be fun to watch if you could see them checking out the deck for any hints of food.

Other birds and animals would leave their clues on the beach too. Occasionally, we would see a beaver swimming by. We also saw the occasional mink and fisher hunting along the water's edge.

The red fox would track alongside of the road looking, listening and smelling for a mouse or mole. In the late spring, a large snapping turtle might even venture out of the trout stream to the sandy edges of the road. At dusk or dawn, it was not unusual to see a deer cross near the edge of the forest.

For a week or two each summer, the forest filled with the enchantment of the twinkling fireflies. These magical creatures would dart on the edge of the woods and sometimes over the meadows with their greenish glow, announcing the coming of summer. These lights of these fairies of the woodlands glow brightly then dim. It was a challenge to catch one in a glass jar to watch them closely. Our time with them in the jar was always brief so we were sure that they could once again rejoin the others who were lighting the dark reaches of the forest.

We were always intrigued by the porcupine. Quills always made a good "show and tell" item to take back to Windsor so we often would try to throw a towel or some fabric over the porcupine in hopes of it sticking some quills into it. On one occasion, the toss of a towel at the beastie up the tree ended up with an unperturbed porcupine that now had a towel to use up in the tree beside him. Woe to the dog that ran into the porcupine. The only one who was in worse shape after a dog has been quilled is the owner of the dog at the vet when he has been billed.

It is only a matter of time before a dog at the cottage would return to the cottage au skunk. That pleasant experience – like the pungent smell – is ingrained in the memory of all who were there.

We would rarely see a coyote or a wolf. But there was a stage when we wished we could have imported a wolf for a week or two. Camp Mini-Yo-We were fine neighbours. However, one year someone had the eco-friendly and cost-recovery concept of keeping pigs at the camp. These pigs would be bought as piglets and then fed the scraps of food leftover by the campers each day. Over the course of the summer they would grow sufficiently to be sold to a farmer or taken to their greater destiny. We did not object to the concept of stewardship that the camp was trying; but we did object to the air pollution these pigs represented. Their fell reek would float from the border of the Mini-Yo-We property toward our road, Rock Island and other areas we used to enjoy with clean, fresh air. We were glad when the experiment ended after a couple of years.

We did see bear at the cottage. Sometimes it was a black bear in the woods or crossing the road. On one occasion, the bear sat down in front of the cottage right beside the camera we had left out during our time in the sun. We were inside. The camera was beside the bear. The bear was not interested in taking its own picture; although it might have been a better shot to record the surprised looks on our faces peering out the cottage windows at the bear.

Once during one of my brother's stay, a bear decided to leave a claw mark ripped into the front door of the cottage.

They may not have enjoyed being there with us but we enjoyed seeing them and knowing that the eyes in the forest might just be watching us.

13. Cottage Types

Muskoka is a place of wonder. In fact there is so much there to explore, experience and enchant that one could spend a lifetime and only just begin to see the beauty of that creation. Part of what makes this so is the many ways that people can experience something new and satisfying.

Some people particularly enjoy the summer months at the cottage. Others cannot wait for the autumn with its quieting pace. Fewer perhaps enjoy the short transition of spring with its rain and bugs but even there the newness of life is amazing. For others the majestic silence of the winter months where so much of nature asleep under the frozen blanket of snow is their favorite time of year. Even within a season, you can have an amazing assortment of lifestyles focused on nature, boating, fishing, canoeing, hiking and so much more.

There is such a variety of types of cottagers. No matter what the era you find people with very different ways of experiencing Muskoka. Our cottage happened to be on the lake. That made us "Lake People." You will find certain characteristics of the people like us who share shoreline next to their neighbors. They tend to be open to impromptu visits from someone on the next beach or dock. This gives a chance to catch up on how life is going. The shared experience of the waterfront invites relationship. The required space between cottages on lakes like Mary Lake means that you will have a short list to get to know at the waterfront.

The "Island People" are an entirely other group. They live with the paradox of isolation – being on an island and yet much more visible than most waterfront cottages as boats and canoes travel by. They also have to contend with the anglers who drop anchor near docks and shallows around their island.

Then there are the "River People" who experience a closeness to the water usually quite dissimilar from the lake people where their property is set back or set high upstairs. The river people also experience the travelers and learn the importance of a wave to the passing boater with the hope that the only waves they send back is with their hand. No wake means something very different to the river cottager and has nothing to do with sleeping. The road people tend to be the year-round citizens who increasingly dot the outlet roads.

Many people have their first encounters with Muskoka through the wonderful children's camps that can be found throughout the district. These are the "Camp People" who know Muskoka through the camping experience. Some of camps are secular; many others include religious heritage often dating back to the 1930s when many such camps were begun across Canada. Camp Mini-Yo-We is on Mary Lake. Camp Widjiitiwin is the children's camp at the Muskoka Bible Centre on the north end of the lake. Campers from nearby Pioneer Camps can be seen walking around in Port, paddling on the lake in canoes and at the Port Sydney Falls.

Others are the "Inn People" introduced to the Muskoka area through a stay at one of the many wonderful inns, resorts, bed and breakfasts or other accommodations in the area. The Cliff House on the southwest corner of the lake and Gryffin Lodge on the eastern shore of Mary Lake have been there for many years. In the distant past, a visit to the Muskoka Lodge not far from the Jackson's property would be your introduction to Mary Lake.

Not to be forgotten are the "Village People" and "Towns People" who have different views of the area and its seasonal inhabitants. They hope to see their incomes swell as their roads are filled by the cottagers who have trekked north to explore life in Muskoka.

Even among visitors to the area you find the distinction between the longtime cottagers and the nouveau families who having conquered some area of business, industry, real estate or entertainment now have carved out a piece of Muskoka for themselves. This is not new but is the history of the area as different generations choose to make Muskoka part of their story. The district has always been a combination that included the rich and those who provided services for them. Regardless of what cottage type you are, Muskoka never failed to enchant those who came to learn of its many faces.

14. Clammed Up

One of the great features of the cottage property was the waterfront. Along the more than 300 feet we enjoyed a large percentage of beachfront that was made up of very unusual red sand. This red sand was part of the remains of the granite that is predominant in the Muskoka area. The red feldspars from the granite gave us a unique beach experience. The consistency of the sand was dense and smooth – almost as thick as clay. One of the other elements found in granite could also be seen in spots along the beach. These black swirls and deposits of mica contrasted with the bright red beach and shallow water. You could also see in spots some of the sparkle from the quartz that also must have been crushed and pulverized before it was deposited by the receding glacier so many years ago.

Being a spring-fed lake with good depth and circulation of water meant that the shallows around our beach were largely clear of vegetation and debris. Added to that was the fact that the shallows were all sand with no rocks to injure tender feet. The shallow waters continued out a long way and included a sandbar some distance out to the south of the main beach. This meant it was a great location for small children to learn the joys of swimming with no surprises from sudden drop-offs or large rocks. Also, because it was shallow, the sun was able to warm the little bay more quickly than usual to the liking of most of those swimming. Those wishing a cooler experience just had to go a little deeper.

There was a sandbar not far to the south where after the water became deeper for a while then really shallow so that at times it was only up to your shins. It felt strange to be so far out yet to stand in such a shallow spot.

More than one motor boat had to be freed from the sandbar as they came too close to our swimming area.

Once you traveled out some distance you began to feel the water rise and by the time you were chest deep, you started to feel the beginning of mud and plant life below. This was affectionately known as "clam-land", as it was the place where you began to encounter large numbers of freshwater clams. Some of these clams were quite adventurous and found their way into shallower water. This was great if you wanted to observe their strange travels that were marked by their trails in the sandy water. It was fun to pick them up and sometimes see them squirt water. Inevitably, some of these clams ended up on the menu of the late-night diners with the suspicious masks. The raccoons and others would wade into the shallow water in search of the clams and enjoy the delicacies on offer. This meant some of the shells were left open on the beach or in the shallows which meant it was a good idea to spend the first few minutes of your swimming time scouting the bottom for any of these characters.

One of the great tragedies from my cottage years dates back to when I was around nine years old. We had just arrived for a number weeks. It had been a long and difficult drive from Windsor to Mary Lake. Our excitement had grown as we passed the various cities and towns that indicated we were closer to our cherished destination. Passing through Port Sydney and surrounding the lake we hit the cottage road and finally the car stopped.

With all the enthusiasm and foolishness of youth we raced into the cottage, grabbed our swimming trunks, changed into them and raced down the many forty-odd stairs to the beach. In a competition to see who could jump in the lake first, I raced forward and just before diving into that marvelous lake, I planted my foot. Pushing off I felt a slicing pain between my big toe and the ball of my foot.

Thankfully, Mary Lake is not home to any sharks or other predators who are motivated by the smell of blood chumming the waters. A quick review of my foot and the gushing blood confirmed my friend the clam not only won that round but also put me out of the lake for two weeks.

Hobbling upstairs, my poor parents who were still settling into the cottage after their long drive of six hours with three cantankerous boys now learned that their eldest son had sliced open his foot and needed to go to the hospital. A number of stitches later, we returned to the cottage where I learned how to watch others swim when I could not.

To this day whenever my wife, Cari, orders clams at a restaurant I am reminded of that clam and that day. In spite of the numerous clams eaten over the years, we are not quite even yet.

15. Mission Impossible

My father grew up in the Great Depression and like many of his generation, his natural instinct was to assume the worst. This was not always a wrong point of view because sometimes the worst did happen. (But that only encouraged him as it proved him right.)

To combat these fears, one of the tactics often used is "The List".

Checklists can be very useful. I am glad to think that the pilots on the planes I fly as a passenger have checklists – and follow them. I am glad to learn that surgeons in many hospitals now also follow a similar checklist before diving in – less surgical error is a good thing.

Cottages are much different than your house or apartment at home. It usually involves experiencing a new and unfamiliar set of circumstances for the cottage novice or visitor. So not surprisingly, a list was born. This list would include in great specificity all of the activities one must do and not do at the cottage. It also comprised where to find things and what to expect in your time there. There are cottagers who are "key" people (with all locks on buildings, boats and other valuables having a key to unlock them) and the people who were sure they would lose the key and opted for the combination locks. Of course, these "combo" people had to live in as much fear of forgetting the combination or the many ways to open a lock (three times around clockwise, two times back forward to the number) and needed to write the combinations everywhere. We were combination people and that meant fighting with locks in all kinds of weather and positions. But the combinations were on the list! This grand list was later expanded into detailed manuals that awaited the newcomers along with the guest book for them to sign. (also on the list!).

One could be quite knowledgeable about the various contingency plans and choices that could be enacted in whatever disaster might be visited upon the cottage and its inhabitants. Anyone studying the manual could easily become an air-raid warden or emergency response worker in the next calamity.

The problem for Dad was that he did not differentiate between those who grew up at the cottage with those who were coming for the first time. So for those of us who might have been considered experienced were reminded of the list before any trip to the cottage no matter how many times we had been there in the preceding week.

"Remember, this is a fuse box – not breakers. Don't put the wrong fuses in the holes. Do not leave the water running. Make sure the toilet is not stuck. Turn out all the lights. Shut off the spotlights on the outside so the animals do not keep turning them on. Turn off the stove." And so it would go.

Going through the list did not actually allay his fears or make him feel better because he was not there to be sure things were really run properly. That was always the catch for him. What he really needed (alas before the technology would have allowed it) was the remote control operation to turn off or on any and every variable at the cottage and a webcam to see what was happening at any time.

It became funny after years of it being an irritation. The call would end with Mom wishing us to have a really great time and Dad giving us the list. It finally helped to think of how Peter Graves would feel as Mr. Phelps in Mission Impossible. No matter how many successful missions he had been on, the taped instructions for the next mission always included "Should you or any of your IM team be captured or killed, the Secretary will disavow any knowledge of your actions. This tape will self-destruct in 5 seconds. Good luck, Jim." Perhaps Dad was an old CIA man in an earlier life. There was always another tape waiting for us before the next visit.

16. Bugged

Paradise has always had its serpents. In the case of Muskoka, it is the bugs. It is a good thing that we had hearty explorers in the early years of Muskoka life. They could have reasonably concluded through a number of the months of the year that it was uninhabitable.

No cottage book would be complete without a first nod to our friends – the swarming black flies. These bugs are so small as to seem like they belong in the fruit fly family. Well fruit flies are to black flies as fruit bats are to their vampire kin. These tiny agents of pain and itch can find the smallest of openings to nibble away at you. If it is May, you are probably praying for a heat wave that will burn off the blackflies. But it is not to be. It was not uncommon to see a family member come in with blood dripping down as though they had just fought a death match out there. But until then, it does not help to say you gave at the office.

Mosquitoes are not unique to cottage life but they seem very good at their game. I think of all the bugs, these ones are the best trained in psy-ops or in long form, psychological warfare. It is not enough that they will take a rainy day and make it worse by being everywhere. They want you to be afraid. Very afraid. The mosquito is willing to do whatever it takes to drive you crazy. A tried and tested method of psy-ops is sleep deprivation. Keep the enemy from sleeping and you can break them sooner. So the mosquito headquarters send in the lone mosquito on a special mission. By buzzing in the cottage all night, you could never really sleep. If you could no longer take the torment and tried to find the lone assassin expect to be disappointed. They can hide behind a curtain, in a crack in the wall or in the next room. Many a seasoned warrior surrendered after one of those nights.

Climbing up the list is the deer flies. These often replace the black-flies burned off by the heat and the mosquitoes that lurk in the woods until the area dries up. Deer flies are quite happy to meet you on the road on a sunny day. They have a distinctive triangular shape and love to get in your hair – literally. They will find a spot and burrow in until they can take a nice chunk out of you with the ouch to go with it. The good news is that they can often be killed before they can get you.

Sometimes you meet a massive horse fly who too will enjoy making their mark on your cottage experience. Like the deer fly, you often can swat them or at least scare them off. You'd better since they can take a nice hunk of flesh as a souvenir.

Worst of all perhaps was the more occasional moose fly. These large black monsters would appear flying over the water at the beach forcing all there to dive under and hold their breath as long as possible to avoid losing a limb. On the rare occasion when we were able to swat one down into the lake, a cheer would go up that would echo around the lake.

The resistance to these creatures was not quite futile but it was some-times funny. We had a bunch of mosquito hats with netting that reached down to cover your head from top to neck to tuck into your coat. We were always a strange site as you encountered another of your intrepid family or friends who were wearing the hats.

A low-tech and eco-friendly solution was to use the large ferns along the road to act as an umbrella and swatter for the deer flies.

We also had our share of wasps and yellow-jacket hornets. The wasps did impress us with the large football sized nests that they would cre-ate and hang on a limb in the forest. More than once, we took our chances to see if you could take the nest as a souvenir.

One of the other creatures that made their presence known were the tent caterpillars. These invaders would be around most years but occasionally they became a plague of Biblical proportions. The worst problem was the way that they deforested the trees. Thankfully, they were usually confined to the odd tent here and there; however, if they were multiplied, it was bad news indeed.

If you were near the lake, you might also have a visit from the dock spider. These beasties look quite formidable with their size and jet-black colouring. We could find them waiting in our boat or on a log near the beach.

The only sure cure for the bugs was the coming of August and then the fall when you could enjoy a wonderful warm day that was bug free. Little wonder that the older folks always said cottage life in the autumn was best.

17. The Waltons

For many generations, time with the extended family happened in the same house (with the boomerang generation what is old becomes new again!) as families lived and grew up with grandparents and grandchildren in the home. As city life developed, some children had the experience of visiting Grandma and Grandpa on the family farm for part of the summer.

The "family farm" experience for us as with many others happened at the cottage. The cottage was a place where grandkids could enjoy extended time with grandparents in a setting of new and different events. I have always believed that it was important for children to develop separate relationships with their extended family in addition to the collective relationships that are developed when the family is together. It is a great gift to get to know your aunt or uncle outside of your parent's direct gaze. So too with grandparents, it is helpful to have time when you can get to know them and they you one on one. I very much valued times I spent with my grandmother and grandfather, Joseph and Lily Fairley. I would go with them on trips or stay over at their house in Windsor.

Our children enjoyed those same experiences with Grandma and Grandpa Fairley at the cottage. They had days together where they could be "grandchildren" rather than being the children. That was important. They learned how to relate to other family adults and appreciate their values – as well as their eccentricities! They created memories together that were separate and distinct from their memories with the entire family.

My mother enjoyed doing projects with children. These included crafts that were fun for different ages. It might be making and painting bird houses – in thanks to the birds for their generous and melodic singing. A sewing project might include a special teddy bear who would now come to life and be added to the family. (One went on to win first prize at one of the local fairs!)

She loved to bake with the children. Whether it was cakes or pies, the results were always tasty. The children became experts in various family cookie recipes. Hello Dollys, Bachelor Buttons, Yule Logs (in season), cut-out shaped sugar cookies decorated with many sparkles and silver balls were great fun to make – and to eat. Grandma especially enjoyed making Gingerbread Men. Sometimes their eyes would be raisins. Sometimes they would be chocolate chip. These were always fashionable GB men as they had well appointed and colourful buttons made of Smarties or M&Ms.

Dad would enjoy having the additional time-saving junior labour as well as the opportunities to impart some of his many tinkering and fix-it skills. These projects often involved some DIY (Do It Yourself) improvements but all were DIN (Do It Now) as my father believed you should never put off until lunch what could be done in the morning. (He never considered putting it off until tomorrow as he liked to say, "Time Is My Enemy.")

Sadly disappointed with his results in teaching me the practical skills he valued, he was still enough of an optimist to hope that the next generation might be better. Indeed, they were as all the children were able to assist Grandpa in both the chores and projects that were part of the cottage experience. Those experiences and his love for them endeared him to them and gave him some additional satisfaction in getting things done.

These experiences are great gifts for children. That is true not only because they learned by doing, but because they learned by doing with their grandparents and other family members along the way. The extended times at the cottage give the generations time to learn from each other and to enjoy the satisfaction of the bonding that can only happen with time well spent.

During the overlap times when there would be many extra people staying over before some would depart, the sleeping arrangements were stretched. As we grew older, the tent outside and later the extra sleeping cabin would help. But in those early days, with the various family members retiring to their rooms, couches and sleeping bags on the floor, you could expect to hear our equivalent to "Goodnight John Boy" The different characters in our story were shouting their goodnights back and forth through the cottage night.

18. The Guest Book

Like many cottages, our cottage had a guest book. Looking at a guest book is always an interesting window on not only the people who visited but also what experiences or moments at the cottage were special to them. All the guests were asked to sign the guest book. If you were a family member present when the guests were visiting, it was your responsibility to ensure any and all visitors sign the book. This was VERY important. (See the chapter on Mission Impossible for greater certainty.)

So little is written down now. For some of us with disgraphia, this is a relief since we spent our school lives being upbraided by most of our teachers who put our illegible handwriting to being a lazy booger (as Major Richard Sharp would call them) or a messy boy which amounts to the same thing. I did have a teacher who was both perceptive and proactive. She was my grade 2 teacher as well as the school art teacher. Mrs. Grayson told my parents at the dreaded parent/teacher conference to "Buy the boy a type-writer." That was around 1966. The typewriter was old, heavy and required great finger strength to plunk down the keys. But from that day onward, when I was allowed to type, I did. When I was not – it was an exercise that was somewhere between hieroglyphics and writing with the ancient Greek alphabet. I was a very early adopter of speech recognition software (IBM ViaVoice) and actually taught it but I digress.

Very few people now write letters by hand. Even fewer people keep a daily journal. So many of the thoughts, dreams, cares and sorrows of life are no longer found in our handwriting. Instead, our digital signature is all that remains with the superficiality of most social network sites like Facebook. Twitter requires the old skill of creating a telegram. Instead of "stop" we now include characters like # and @ within the messages. How do you say something meaningful in a line or two? If you are gifted at that, you'll be creating memorable quotes before long. It is much easier to boil down the sap of sugar maple trees when making maple syrup with my friends Murray and Barb Knights. But like others, I too will try to keep my Twitter account active, if not busy.

But there was a time when it was only letters sent to friends and family far away that would allow you to communicate all the things that were important for them to know. In doing so, you told them a great deal about yourself and your life – even if these were the tales of everyday life. Letters and journals are rich veins to mine when trying to understand the past of family members or a culture.

So the guest book remains one of the few non-cyber trails to say, "I was here." In the simple record of the fact of the visit, you begin to have a sense of the many people who walked through the cottage door to share a visit for a day or a week at Mary Lake.

Consistent with their personalities (or if the unsigned guest book was remembered as they were walking out the door!), some people merely include their names and the date. Others will give you what could have been an early version of the Tweet. Their words include a thankyou and a phrase of delight or satisfaction. Some perhaps are not used to writing such notes and so they find the stress of choosing the right words too much and default to the "great time" comment. Others seemed to have noted the pattern of notes above and tried to be in keeping with the trends of how many words were used.

Then there were others who took the opportunity to reflect in the book like a true journal as they recounted special moments and opportunities to enjoy the unique times in Muskoka. For some of the guests, you sensed it was a refuge from a very busy life. For others, they had been welcomed into a home away from home for some comfort during trying times.

So, if you get to enjoy looking back on a cottage guest book, you will discover many things. In the most basic sense, you will see that just as they left their marks on the pages, the cottage experience had left its mark on them too.

19. That's Entertainment

In the age when landfills were more or less self-serve, you would round up your un-composted garbage and take a trip to the dump. If some of your cottage worthy items where revealed to no longer being cottage worthy, their designation was changed to "Dump Worthy" and would be parked by the car or van for the next trip to the dump.

If you did not actually do "dump runs" in the sixties and seventies in Muskoka, you might wonder how you could convince someone to leave the beauty of the cottage to go to a refuse pile. That is because you have missed the entertainment factor that all the dumps included – free of charge!

Our dump was usually on a road off South Mary Lake Road. That meant that many of the villagers from Port Sydney would also make their visits there.

The first thing to do upon arrival at the dump was to have a tossing contest. Each of the young teens would grab a garbage bag and wind up for a mighty throw into the pit. Who could throw it the farthest? Whoever lost was sure to blame it on the weight differential of the bags. Too heavy was short. Not enough weight to carry it far – excuses for the same bag that lost the toss. After the stinky garbage was away, you positioned your vehicle to be out of the way of other cars while maintaining a good vantage point of the large pit. (It was also wise to be upwind of the pit if you did not wish to singe your nostrils.)

Comfortably seated, you would sit back and watch the parade of people who would come to dump their items. I am not sure whether it was better suited as a study in sociology or a missing episode of Candid Camera but it was always entertaining.

Some people were clearly anxious to hit and run. They raced in and practically without stopping the bags or other items were heaved into the pit. Others seemed to treat this as some type of funeral procession as they slowly entered the area. They would carefully take the newly designated dump-worthy items out of their car with great reverence. Then the procession would slowly take them to the designated area or pit. They would look forlornly at the item as they held it for the last time – as if some last minute reprieve might return the item to cottage worthy status. But without the call from the governor to stay the execution, they would let the item fall from their hands into its final resting place. Standing still in a moment of silent reflection on the many years of service the item had provided, they finally moved. Then pausing as if they were going to pick up some dirt and cast it into the pit they sadly turned to their car and drove off.

You could learn a great deal from the scroungers. With the same industry (and apparently lack of a sense of smell) as dung beetles, these industrious characters were constantly hanging around the dump. Some were in search of an item that could be scrapped for money. Many others were there in search of something interesting to take home with them. Sheds, garages and basements were full of these treasures found by people who wanted to give them another chance. You could always recognize these "previously dumped" items because they were a bit like zombies. You think you know what they once were but you are quite sure they should not be where they are now. Sadly, some of these kinds of items occasionally found their way to the shed at the cottage. Looking back perhaps, it was not just a coincidence that Dad and the daytime dump supervisor were on a first name basis.

But the real fun at the dump was to watch for the arrival of the animals at dusk. A wide variety of critters would come to share the spoils. On a good night, you would get to see the greatest scroungers of them all – the black bears. Better than a visit to the zoo, you could enjoy watching them wander around the dump boosting their bad cholesterol. On one occasion, a group of us in our twenties had to take a now "dump worthy couch" to its final resting place. It was loaded into the van with the rest of us. Once there (and it being dusk) we decided to set up for the show. One last time the couch was called into service as we set it up to watch the Muskoka bear show. Not wanting to disappoint these friends gathered from as far as Mississippi, the bears came out. There gathered on the couch was a group of highly educated spectators cheering the bears on. After the show, the faithful couch was added to the dump. But what a way to go. Cheering friends and a bunch of bears with a Muskoka sunset every couch should be so lucky as it finishes its service!

20. For the Birds

One of the joys of the cottage was the wide variety of birds who would visit as well as the year-round birds who considered us the visitors. Those who are migrating en route to destinations north or south would charm us with their distinctive calls and serenades.

No Muskoka cottage is complete without the haunting sounds of the loon. We had the privilege of seeing many loons drift by. While it was always delightful to hear their call, it was especially at night when the sound of their cries would carry on the wind around the lake. The lake was big enough that you could never be assured of a "loon spotting" on any particular day so when it happened no matter whether you were in the canoe, on the beach or in the motorboat, it was magical. It was always a game to scan the lake when the loon submerged and spot where it would resurface.

The loons shared their domain with their more populous and less appreciated cousins, the seagulls. While the book, "Jonathan Livingston Seagull" seemed for a time to enhance their reputation and they are now more closely associated with parking lots at McDonald's. However, those who live on the lake earned some respect because they maintained the illusion at least of living off nature rather than on French fries.

Large populations of seagulls, especially at night, inhabited some of the islands. Their cries also could carry across the lake adding to the chorus of other sounds we could hear. Some of the high cliffs on the islands would contain various perches that seemed to be occupied by sentries and seagull nobility. Their presence could also be seen by the white stain flowing down the cliffs. Some of the cliffs were sufficiently white as to make us think of Vera Lynn singing about the bluebirds. We never did quite figure out whether the seagulls are generally cooperative with one another or are just incapable of keeping a secret. If you are fishing and one of the fish did not survive removing the hook (as rarely happened), it never took long before the floating fish was spotted by a seagull even though there appeared to be none around. Not content to enjoy their meal, the seagulls often spent their time squawking that they had sighted the meal. They made such a noise that they were soon joined by many other comrades who of course were quite happy to be competitors.

Some of the friendliest birds were the cheerful chick-a-dees who would appear and disappear in the cedars and pines. They were regular visitors to the bird feeders as were the blue-jays, cardinals and nuthatches when they were not busy running upside down on a nearby tree. Occasionally a cedar waxwing might visit as well.

We could count on a variety of woodpeckers with the redheaded woodpecker being most likely to tap on the trees near the cottage. Down in the stream area by the beaver dam we had the huge pileated woodpeckers who built their large apartment like nest holes in the old dead trees trapped in the pond.

The hummingbirds were very happy to visit one of grandma's many feeders whenever the bees and yellow-jackets were not too busy there. These tiny birds became quite comfortable with the comings and goings of the cottage. A magical moment for us one summer day was when a hummer ran into a window facing the deck. It was stunned and fell to the ground. Cari carefully got a cloth and picked it up fearing the worst. She sat with the little bird unconscious in her hand for more than ten minutes when suddenly it stood up and then flew off. A happy tale for all concerned.

Just as they do in the north of Scotland, the crows and ravens seem to fit life in the Canadian Shield. Hearing these birds with their mournful or scolding cries carried on the air reminds you of a more primitive time and place. My grandfather Fairley had a favourite fallen log beside the road where he would sit just before Rock Island on our road. He would call out to the crows and before long would have one or more engaged in a conversation. The ravens were something seen more in Algonquin than at the cottage. Their size reminded us why it would not be wise to have a tiny dog romping around the cottage.

My favourite bird earned its place in my heart not from its beauty or habits but from its song. The white-throated sparrow calling with its rising and falling song gently crossing across the meadows of Muskoka meant we were in God's country.

21. Well – Well – Well

Water is an essential part of life anywhere but it can be especially challenging in the remote areas that exist on the Canadian Shield with
its powerful rock so close to the surface. Where and how you sourced your
water was an important early decision.

Some cottages use a combination of lake or river water for everything but their drinking and cooking. The drinking water is brought in jugs or
bottles.

Our cottage went through a series of three wells over the years of
our life there. The first was located just above the beach dug down to source
one of the many underground springs and the high water table that existed so
close to the lake encased in a cement cylinder. This water was pulled by an
ancient and noisy pump up the cliff into the holding tank located under the
cottage. When you first arrived for the season, it was important to run the water for quite a while to get the well refreshing itself. It was not uncommon to
see some sand in the sink or at the bottom of the toilet bowl in the early days.

The early wells also had the risk of temporarily running dry if you
put too many demands on it too quickly. It made you conscious of how important water was to everyday life and how to be a steward of that resource
like many others. It was a contrast to city life where often little thought is
given to the flow of water or other essentials so easily enjoyed.

Eventually, the first well became unreliable and so a new well was
dug in the woods south of the cottage. This well was about 60 feet down and

a place we as children were not allowed to visit. While it had a cement lid, it was a dangerous place. One of the important families in the area was the Hughes family. Doug Hughes was one of those people who seemed to know everyone and could fix anything. He was always the one who would come to help open the cottage by having the water on which included ensuring the well was functioning. I understand that this included hanging upside down to turn on and off a valve in the well as part of winterizing the plumbing.

It was in our later years at the cottage that we entered the world of the drilled wells. Many cottagers knew the horror stories of different attempts to drill that came up dry or with water pressure that was too weak to support the cottage. Over 200 feet later, we had our water source that would transform our water access.

The hard water found deep in the rocks had a great deal of iron in it so we came to learn about the benefits and aggravations of iron filters. No matter how carefully the backwash timer was set for some gentle hour of the day, it often seemed to delight in going off in the middle of the night with a great gushing sound sure to wake the poor souls sleeping next to the panel where it was hidden.

Since we were not a winterized dwelling, any visits outside of the freeze free months when the cottage was open meant that you would need to bring water up from the lake in large buckets. Our hearts were probably in their best condition during those days of bringing the water up stair after stair until we reached the top. Any power outages immediately shut down your water supply so even in the good months, you might have to visit the lake to carry up water to keep the toilets working after a bad storm. We were at the cottage during the great blackout of 2003 when much of the U.S. northeast and the Great Lakes region lost power in that cascading event on a beautiful, storm free summer day. As you would during such unknown events, we listened to a radio report about the event with great uncertainty on how long it might last. We joined the many others who made the drive around the lake to Port to get some water and ice to keep life for children and grandparents going for the duration.

In the early years of the dug wells and following the all clear from our annual water health tests at the opening of the cottage, we would look forward to many tall glasses of great tasting Muskoka well water. Like so many things in cottage life, the progress of the much more efficient and powerful drilled well could never replace the simple and clean taste of the water we had known in simpler times.

22. Measuring Up

A cottage is where history is made and remembered over the generations fortunate enough to call it "home away from home." Guest books, initials carved in wood and the various items accumulated in the cottage all speak to the history of the people and times that are part of the story there. Like rings of a tree, they remember the times that were.

One of our traditions was the measuring board. The practice began at the old log cabin down by the lake nearer the Jackson's main cottage. This place had been rented by the family over many summers beginning in the late 1930s. The old board had on it the names of the different first generation family members with their heights marked and year inscribed. In addition to Lois and Harry were Aunt Joan and Uncle George and Aunt Caylee who had a career in nursing. She and her late husband Graham Bailey lived for many years in Port Rexton, Newfoundland before moving to Alberta. The board was a "We were here!" statement characteristic of human kind who wish to have a remembrance of their life and times.

A new board began at the cottage on the doorframe of Mom and Dad's where we would mark both another year at the cottage along with how much we had grown over the intervening year. With our back straight and with no tippy toes, the pencil would cross over the top of our head to mark the spot that told us how tall we were. It was always very competitive to see where each brother was at the changing ages. We would learn the art of estimation as we tried to conclude how tall each of us were for the number of months we were old. Who would become the tallest of the three boys when the growing stopped? As first-born, my marks were the ones to beat. Not long into my teenage years, I had to cede my height advantage first to middle brother Brian and then finally to youngest brother John.

Eventually, my mother found one of the commercially available height boards with the useful sliding height feature that would sit on your head while Grandma would measure the height and mark the year for each of the youngest generation. This was the board that required the grandchildren to stand at attention each year while Grandma would make the year official.

As kids, we thought of the board measuring our heights. As adults, we realized that what was really being measured – and treasured – was the passing of time together with the additions and losses that time brings.

23. Slip Sliding Away

There are many "rites of passage" that are observed in each culture. These are signposts on the journey to adulthood and beyond in the lives of young women and men. Depending on where you lived, these rites often involved showing some special courage or skill that helped mark your transition from being a boy to a man or a girl to a woman. In the cottage culture, we had a number of such passages.

On the lake, early on it was swimming deeper and deeper in the lake. Later it would be paddling the canoe. Eventually you might be able to steer the motor boat and turn up the throttle. Walks down the darkened cottage road also came in stages until you could face the darkness alone. Eventually you could graduate from setting the fire ingredients in place to where you could actually light the match to start it.

One of the ultimate tests of courage was to join the many teens who were sliding down the falls at Port Sydney. Just after the locks at the south end of Mary Lake was a gift from the Creator – a rapid rush of water that would flow over a rock slope smoothed over the centuries. To get from the top to the bottom was much more challenging than it sounds.

The first hurdle was to get to the top of the falls. This meant walking across the current in water that depending on the time of year could be one to two feet deep. Slowly you would edge your way across trying ever so hard to keep your footing on the sometimes mossy rock below. To go down too soon was to end up in the eddy right beside the rocks where the younger children would sit waiting for their ascension to the big falls. It would be a humiliating defeat. So it was critical to keep your balance and strength long enough to get into the middle of the rock face below.

Once in position, you had to sit down. Once you proceeded a little further, the rock face below would meet bathing suit (not a good idea, as these rocks were great at chewing up traditional suits) or jean shorts (a much better idea). You would skid or slide down the rock bumping and sliding over the rushing water that was now filled with light, bubbles and spray as you bounced down the falls. The ridges of the falls kept you from going too fast and depending on your weight or center of gravity, you could steer a bit to the left or right.

As you saw the bottom of the falls rising to meet you, you braced for a grand moment. The swirling and cresting water would greet you with a flood of bubbles as the journey ended with a good dunking under the flow. Almost immediately, you surfaced with the current taking you over a very shallow series of rocks and stones that became more and more shallow until you could easily stand up. The natural wonder ride was over.

The long walk to the far edge of the pool and then the climb over the many expansive and flat rock faces meant walking over this area to the east. It was usually inhabited with people of all shapes and sizes that came to resemble a staging area for walrus and seals. They were all enjoying their place in the sun.

The better way involved another test of man (or woman) vs. nature. We would slide to the bottom of the falls, find our foothold and begin our very slow and deliberate ascent up the falls. Carefully planting one foot, the other foot would reach forward seeing a spot to press down without too much of a slippery cover. One false step and down you would go, spinning onto your back and sliding into the rapids waiting to consume you with bubbles. This usually would also bring a chuckle from the seals and walrus types watching from the side. But if you persevered and kept your nerve, before you new it, you had climbed all the way up the falls. If you dared to look down, you would see the water rushing over your feet and ankles as the water parted on either side of your foot. It was so cool.

The truly experienced could even lie down halfway on the falls and hold their position with the water flowing over you, trying ever so hard to whisk you down to the bottom of the falls below.

On your first time on the falls, it was a boy who entered the water but it was a man (or something closer to it) who emerged from the journey with the story and adrenalin to match.

The falls had been conquered.

Then at the top again, it was time to take your seat and prepare to slip slide away over the best river ride ever created.

24. Something's Fishy

As we entered our teenage years, it was clear that the occasional sunfish and rock bass were no longer going to be a sufficient challenge for us, in out quest for fish early in the morning. Unless we were at a dock or in the shallows around Dead Man's, Crown or Theodore Island, we found it very difficult to consistently catch any fish. In fact, we were more likely to catch a cold than a fish most evenings.

Growing up, we had always seen on the cottage wall one of those Ministry of Natural Resources maps that indicated what lakes had what species of fish. Mary Lake always had several species identified including lake trout, largemouth bass, smallmouth bass, and pike. So we found it curious that in our many hours spent fishing with a variety of lures and baits that we could not capture any of these marvelous fish.

If you are like us, your tackle box accumulated over many years (and generations) with a wide assortment of lures and other fishing paraphernalia. Some of the lures were fascinating while others were just plain hideous. It made you wonder who bought what lure on what occasion and whether it was out of a sense of humor or desperation that any particular lure was chosen. Along with the lures, you would also have a wide range of split shot and other sinkers, tools such as pliers and knives, leaders and my childhood favorites, bobbers. One of the strangest lures that we had was gray and furry. It was as long as your finger with many different sets of hooks hidden within the fur. We were never quite sure what that lure was made of – it is probably just as well that we did not!

One day as I drove into the nearby town of Bracebridge, I decided to stop into one of the local bait stores called The Minnow Man. As you entered the small store, you could immediately see a wall full of hooks, sinkers and lures. In the window, there were a variety of fishing rods and tackle boxes. Beyond the counter were a series of tubs with bubbling water and swimming minnows. The first tank had the smallest minnows and each tank included larger minnows. By the time you are at the final tank, the minnows were of sufficient size as to remind us of less successful fishing adventures of our own. Then there was a refrigerator that had the word WORMS posted on it.

From the back of the store came John Cooper, a tall weathered man who reminded me of Jack Palance who played Curly in the Billy Crystal City Slicker movies. As he sauntered towards me, I found myself taking a deep breath. I wondered how this man of the woods and lakes would take my question. Such was my frustration at not being able to catch fish regularly that I was able to summon the necessary courage to ask the big question. I told him that I had been fishing on Mary Lake for many years and could only seem to catch rock bass and sunfish. I assured him that I had spent many hours over many years trying all different kinds of bait and lures early in the morning and late at night. I confirmed that I had braved many drizzling mornings and evenings. I spoke of wind directions and various cloud patterns so that my lack of success was not be confused with total ignorance.

I braced for his reply. "Your problem he said is that you are using bait. You should never use bait on Mary Lake." I wondered at that point if both of my legs had suddenly fallen asleep. I could not feel anything in either leg but was certain that he was tugging on at least one of them. He had to be pulling my leg to make such a statement. After the eloquent moment of stunned silence, I asked him to repeat that. Once again, he assured me that we should not use bait on Mary Lake.

It was my turn to take the bait, so I asked, "How do you fish then?" "You don't use bait he said – you use leeches." Now I was thoroughly confused – a familiar sensation for me when it comes to fixing things.

I replied that we swim in the lake and that we would not want to have more bloodsuckers. He said that leeches were not bloodsuckers.

I don't recall whether I responded with a "huh?" or "eh?" but either way he understood my skepticism. He brought a jar with some gooey black creatures climbing up the side. The lid was securely tightened. Next, he grabbed a Styrofoam container filled with water and a dozen similar creatures curled in the water.

He opened the jar, pulled out one of the characters, and put it on the table. He reached into the other container and pulled out one of the curled inhabitants. He went on to say that leeches and bloodsuckers are not the same. Bloodsuckers lived in the shallow waters near the shore and sometimes even out of the water as they waited for unsuspecting animals and people to come into range. Without a lid on their container, the bloodsuckers would escape. He told me to press down on the bloodsucker with my finger. As I did, I could feel that it was very soft like jelly. He then went on to explain that leeches were not found along the shoreline but instead preferred living in the lake. He had me hold one of the leeches in my hand. I braced for the sensation of it digging into my skin for a blood sample and was relieved when it failed to do so. Instead, it would cling but that was all.

The Minnow Man then pronounced his pearl of wisdom. "Fish on Mary Lake with leeches at high noon on a sunny, calm day." Wow!

He explained further that leeches are not food for smallmouth bass but instead are its natural enemy. The leeches are recognized by the smallmouth bass as a danger to their egg beds. Therefore, any time a smallmouth bass recognizes a leech it will attack it. As Mary Lake is a healthy lake with excellent water exchange and flow, it is full of many rich food sources for the fish. To try to compete with those natural sources is extremely difficult. So rather than trying to drop a better worm, dangle a better lure or wiggle a better minnow, you have to take a completely different approach. I asked why the weather conditions and time of day were opposite of the conventional fishing wisdom. He said that because you are wishing the fish to see the leech then having conditions such as, water and bright sunshine improve the odds.

I was impressed. I was not sure that I believed him, but I was quite sure that I had just heard a great fishing tale. That was certainly worth investing in a couple of dozen leeches to try it out for ourselves.

He went on to give me the specific instructions of what size hook, line and sinker to use. He also demonstrated how to hook the leech in such a way that it could swim naturally. What was most remarkable to me was that unlike fishing with a worm where you had to take great pains to ensure that the worm covered the hook, the hook was very visible through the leech.

We readied the old aluminum boat for our expedition. It was unclear whether this would be fishing fortune or folly. We were self-conscious as we made our way to Dead Man's Island with our fishing net blowing in the wind in the bow and our fishing lines strewn on either side of the boat. At a minimum, we were sure that we would bring a smile to the faces of the old-timers who saw these young whippersnappers heading out on a bright sunny day at high noon to catch fish.

It was an eerie feeling to reach into the container of leeches. It really seemed like something out of a horror movie to be that close to that many bloodsuckers. As a compromise, we brought along some fabric gloves from Canadian Tire to hold onto the critters. With the leeches on, we made our first casts. As the plop of the leech hitting the water faded and the line slowly drifted down we wondered what would happen next.

To our surprise and delight, we began to feel the intermittent tugs that he had told us to expect. Unlike conventional bait fishing where the bait is swallowed by the fish, this kind of attack was to kill the leech not eat it. Therefore, the fish would crunch it several times to damage it and then spit it out. As it was crunching the leech, you had to set the hook and slowly start to bring the bass in. This took a little bit of practice. But before long, we began to recognize the feeling of the line during an attack and how to set the hook successfully.

That afternoon we caught the limit. These were all excellent sized smallmouth bass that for anyone who has ever caught one represents one of the most energetic and hard fighting fish pound for pound of any fish you would like to catch.

My greatest fish story was an afternoon at Dead Man's Island. It was while I was still using the small #5 hook and a leech that I felt my line freeze like I had caught a rock. (A familiar if dreaded feeling around the islands.) It then started to feel more like a log that was gradually pulling up. Resisting the temptation to try to snap or cut the line free, I kept reeling it up slowly. Then I felt the line pull back. What was going on? This was not the pull and tug of the energetic bass. After more than ten minutes of battling, the log appeared. It was a pike! How it never bit through the low-test line is still a mystery. I was very glad for the fish net as we hauled the beastie into the boat. My one and only pike was thirty-two inches long. Who knows what can happen when you fish for smallmouth bass?

Over the years that followed, it was no longer a challenge to catch fish. Instead, it was the luxury of catching big fish. Even more satisfying were the many opportunities to take out children and teens (and adults!) who had never caught before and watch the joy they experienced in catching such exciting fish. Needless to say, we were enthusiastic and faithful customers of John Cooper, that rugged and wily old fisherman, the Minnow Man of Bracebridge.

25. Don't Let the Rain Come Down!

Back in the 1960s, a group called the Serendipity Singers introduced the world to a cute song about a crooked man who walked a crooked mile but who was very anxious not to have any rain come down. As you get older, you learn to not only accept but also actually enjoy the changing weather and seasons. A rainy day at the cottage can mean catching up on some reading, a craft or artwork or maybe some sleep. The sound of the rain on the cottage roof can be very enchanting. The rustling and tapping of the leaves by the raindrops creates a gentle ambience to relax even the most stressed person. The two main reasons why you would not want to have it rain at the cottage are children and leaks. It is hard to say which one of the two is more frustrating. However, for most of the old-time cottage owners we have all been there.

The leaks can be very disturbing particularly when they occur at night and there is little to be done to stop them. With the extremes of heat and cold and the buffeting of windstorms in Muskoka, many roofs experience a very sudden failure in spite of our best inspections and intentions. That usually means that we have to resort to pots. Usually when one leak has occurred, it is soon joined by a few others. So the pots that had been making porridge in the morning or boiling hot dogs in the afternoon are now on the floor catching the drips with the ping, ping, ping of the torture chamber. These roof failures are often able to coincide with the end of the vacation when dollars and time are scarce.

But as challenging as a leaky roof can be, nothing will test the soul of the old-time cottage dweller than a rainy day with kids. If you can remember back to a time before cottages had the Internet, satellite TV, Blu-ray DVDs, Xbox PS3 and Wii, then you can remember the extra challenges of rainy day kids. Those were the years when board games saved what little sanity was left for parents. Snakes and ladders, Parcheesi, crokinole, checkers, chess and cards were the entertainment. Some games that seem to take forever to play such as Monopoly and Risk were perfect for the rainy day. We all honed our skills by passing the damp hours playing our favorite games. As a new generation is rediscovering an interest in the simplicity of board games, some of us are enjoying a return to those old past times which our parents understood as tools to pass time. We especially enjoyed playing Stock Ticker and Rumoli by the hour. There were times we could even enjoy doing a puzzle.

It was quite a revolution for us when the Atari 2600 came out. With simple graphics and basic challenges we could play not only on a rainy day away but also lose ourselves in competition with the opposition during a perfectly sunny day when we should have been enjoying the great outdoors. Whether it was defender, baseball, space invaders, asteroids and of course Pac-Man, the forerunners of current technology snatched their first generation. The addition of VHS tapes and more television channels ensured that the frustrations and pains of the rainy day disappeared.

Once the early personal computers were available, it became a new problem to pack the car already full with one of the X-Cargo snail tops strapped to the roof. Now space had to be found for those grand bulky computers like the IBM PS2 (our first) with the large monitors and the very small memories. If the already too small car looked overfilled – the discussion among the kids was what parent to leave behind to ensure that the computer came for the weeks there. Truth is, I enjoyed the many hours of Bards Tale, Earl Weaver Baseball, Pirates' Gold and those other early software titles. Rainy days were never the same again!

26. Look Up – Way Up!

There are castle doors on Mary Lake – or at least on the north branch of the Muskoka River.

They are not the castle doors of The Friendly Giant or Hogwarts. These are the tall castle-like doors of the locks that connect boaters on Mary Lake with Fairy Lake, Peninsula Lake, Lake Vernon and the rest of the Lake of Bays.

As you head north on Mary Lake, passing the Muskoka Bible Camp, you enter the North Branch of the Muskoka River. It narrows quickly as you pass many river cottages and river people who might be sitting on their docks fishing or enjoying the sun. Sometimes you would encounter some children swimming. There was usually a tree or two with a long rope to allow those brave enough to fly through the air before their big splash.

The river would then become quiet again as you approached Camp Widjiitiwin on the west side. You would have sections that were farmland with the occasional cow staring at you while you puttered by in the motor boat and they enjoyed a cool drink. Other shorelines would include bush with a variety of trees. Not quite the bayous of Louisiana – no Spanish moss – but still an intimate trip. Depending on the time of year, you might also meet a family of ducks. Occasionally it was mallards but more often, it would be wood ducks that would seem to parallel your course and then suddenly veer off to a safer shore.

After what seemed like a long series of twists and turns you would encounter an opening within sight of Muskoka Road 2 as it carried people into Huntsville. There was a small picnic area under what is traditionally one of the most colourful trees in the autumn. Then you were getting close.

Soon your boat was in the straight heading for those big doors. Look up – way up! At the top, you might see some fellow travelers who had left their boats while waiting to come through on their way to Mary Lake. Sometimes you would see some people who had just stopped by the road to watch the locks in operation.

When the water was released from the locks, the great doors would open and in your boat would go. It might be a solo trip or there might be other boats that had arrived at the same time as you. You would pick a side of the locks where you could grab on to one of the plastic covered chains that hung down from the top. When the lock keeper was ready, they would push on the wooden lever with their full weight to swing the lock doors shut.

Next, they would release the other side to allow the water to fill the lock raising you and all the others going for the ride up. Holding on to the chains you would keep yourself at the side to avoid the current pushing past the boat as the water filled the lock. After about ten minutes, the water would be equalized and your boat would be level with the side of the lock. After handing over your nominal lock fee to the teenager or retiree lock keeper (never seemed to be anything in between) the big door would open on the other side and you would continue on your way.

Winding along the rest of the journey, you would go under the Highway 2 bridge that crossed the river and head around the twists and turns until you came to the opening to Fairy Lake. Then it was off to Huntsville to the west or Peninsula Lake and beyond to the east.

It was not the fastest way to get to Huntsville but it was the most memorable for young and old alike. Although the old usually complained of a small motor boat condition known as "mesattoolongandgotnumbbum." All aboard were glad to reach the restrooms.

27. Many Wanderings

The cottage road represented a place of solitude for the one wishing the quiet walk with only the sounds of nature for company. For us of the small boy variety, it was the beginning of adventures where we could go further and further on our own, as our courage would allow. Our part of the road at that time led only to our cottage so there was no traffic unless it was a family member who usually was hunting for the children for lunch or swim. In an area halfway up the road you could veer to the north through an opening in the woods and find a special place we called Rock Island. This outcropping of Canadian Shield surrounded by large green ferns provided a great spot for picnics and play. It also could be a road for exercise or conversation. Over the years, some of the more prominent boulders and rocks at the sides of the road were named in honor of the various children. They usually had to endure a picture or two of them perched on their rock over the course of the summer.

Fort Rock was located to the north of Doug and Beth Rocks in the woods about five minutes up. You would walk out of the thick woods to a large open area – like a meadow within the woods – where it was flat and grassy with some rock outcrops. It was a spot where you expected to see some deer standing with their fawns sleeping nearby. It was very peaceful. But given the size, it might have been just right for an Entmoot. Forests as nice as our area must have had some Treebeard types keeping it beautiful. Ents. That's it!

Family walks often included one or more of the group going ahead to hide in the trees like Sylvan elves or Rangers of the North hoping to not be seen or heard by the others who were wandering on the way. Only after the others had passed by would the silent watches appear behind the group with a giggle or a shout to announce their success.

Walks down the road also varied with the seasons. The spring walks were lush. The summer walks were dry and dusty. The fall walks were peaceful as if the road itself was at rest. The winter walks were so very quiet except for the passing call of a crow. Each season shared the journey with you as you passed along the way.

Night walks would allow you to enter another world. If you turned off your flashlight (or as often happened, when the flashlight went off due to dead batteries) you were in utter darkness. If you were on the part of the road where the forest was on either side, you could not see the hand in front of your face. Deprived of your sense of sight, your other senses would be heightened. This was great if you were attempting to take in the night noises. It was a test of nerves if you heard something else wandering through the sticks and leaves not far away. The reward of the walks along the dark road would be the times when you could gaze up into the heavens. The many stars and the bright moon were enchanting on a clear night.

The road also represented a rite of passage for the various children. At some point when they were brave enough, we would do a midnight walk down the road from one end to the other with a flashlight and a parent. The hurried and nervous conversation on the journey from the cottage grew more relaxed as we would return. The next stage was to make the same walk together without a flashlight. Lions and tigers and bears, O my! That was tough too. Then their final test, often years later, was to make the midnight journey on their own. We are happy to report that nearly all the children have returned.

28. Please Pass the Salt

The first encounters with the cold water that is Mary Lake in May when you are opening the cottage became a rite of passage and a proof of either courage or insanity. While the shallows might have hints of warming up, the fact that this lake was over two hundred feet deep in its trough meant that there was a great deal of cold water to circulate to any part that was warming up too soon. You could be forgiven for believing the lake sensed your approach and altered the cold current to meet your every step.

Depending on the task, your valour might be tested for a short time in putting out the motor boat or for a much more grueling experience like anchoring the raft in water that might be chest high or worse. The numbing would spread from toes to feet to legs and beyond as duty called. As teens, we often wondered how these experiences might influence our ability to have children later in life. Four children later, I was able to reassure others later in life that this was not an excuse that could be used to avoid the experience.

The same exercises had to be done in reverse as you joined the many other cottagers who would sadly submit to the calendar in October and the rituals of saying goodbye to the cottage as part of the Thanksgiving weekend. We always had special sympathy for those who had long docks that would be brought up for the winter months. Ugh!

Among the additional tasks of the opening days would be to wander through the shallow water in search of clams or other debris that might injure the children and anyone else wandering in the lake. Over the winter, it was not uncommon to find logs and smaller groups of sticks that had been caught

by the small bay that protected our beach and gave us such ideal wading
depths for children to enjoy.

One of the reasons that we would seek out the logs and sticks was
to ensure that none of the dreaded hitchhikers had attached themselves to
the wood. These creatures float on submerged wood or even on the shoreline waiting for an unsuspecting warm-blooded victim to stand nearby. They
would slide over to you and find a spot on your foot, leg or arm to begin rasp-
ing through your skin and filling themselves with your blood. The dreaded
bloodsuckers were something you tend to encounter sooner or later in most
of the northern lakes. But once you have seen yourself as the prey rather than
the predator, you are quite willing to take away the easy meals for the vam-
pires of the shallows.

Fortunately for us, the shallows around our area was very sandy and
clear so it did not lend itself to being good blood sucker territory compared
to cottages that were closer to the mouth of rivers and streams where they
would live as well.

If you have ever had one of these blood suckers attach to you, your
panicked reaction like most people is to try to pull, tear or scrape it off. You
learn that while this can remove the beastie, it leaves you with a bleeding
hole where it was before being interrupted while dining. In the days when
more people smoked and carried lighters, some would put flame to blood
sucker forcing it to become some kind of mutant escargot for a passing fish.

The tried and true method that most experienced cottages relied on
was the saltshaker. Enough salt applied generously to the bloodsucker would
cause it to withdraw and wither leaving you with just a horrible memory and
not a bleeding site on your limb. Truth be told – there was probably some
sense of righteous satisfaction of a salt judgment being delivered upon the
evil creature.

So if you see a saltshaker at the beach do not assume that it is for
the celery or other snacks that might be enjoyed there. And if someone says,
"Please pass the salt" you will know that now means now. In fact – very
now-now!

29. Ahoy There

Communication at the cottage was a challenge in the early days. As mentioned elsewhere, the phones were rotary and on a party line for many years. There were no cell phones or car phones to chat or text. The public internet was still far off.

Instead, there were various ways to communicate with the scattered children. In the early years, it was an old bell fixed on a wall inside the screened porch. Pulling down on the short leather rope would create a good ding that could be heard most of the time to announce lunch or supper. But if the wind was blowing off the lake and up the hill, you could hear everything going on at the beach but the beach could not hear you over the wind and the waves. You would need a messenger to climb down the many stairs to convey the message with the real risk that the messenger would be distracted by the temptations to swim or play with the others who already having fun. It sometimes meant that you ran out of younger people to convey the message before any word came back. Little wonder that Mom often gave up and just brought lunch down for a picnic on the beach or the rocks.

Communicating the other way was equally challenging. Sound could carry well if the wind was blowing up onto the land. However, it became impossible to hear any responses. It was a useful learning experience about the importance of declarations or imperatives vs. interrogatory sentences. To ask a question was to plan on frustration because you would never hear the answer. So figure out what needed to be communicated. Say it as a fact. In an emergency – do not bandy your words about. Otherwise, it might be you who is climbing the stairs.

After a trip to Switzerland, I brought back a decorative animal horn that was equipped to make a hideous sound. It was occasionally used to break through the din of other noises. I would have preferred an alpenhorn. It would have echoed well off the rocks and hills around but it was a bit big to bring back. We also thought of bagpipes – fitting for this highland area on property owned by Scots but as none of us had a set, it was just a passing thought. Perhaps just as well since not all neighbours may have welcomed the sound of the pipes on the lake. Bagpipes are one of those instruments that make either your heart rise or your temper flare.

It was a big deal when transistors became cheap and we could have our first (of many) pairs of walkie-talkies. The range was always terrible in those early models but it was cool to be able to at least beep each other. It would never carry well over the cliff to the beach or very far down the road. The batteries also did not last long so you could not leave them on which rather defeated the purpose. When they were on, often you could hear the person speaking nearly as well with the volume off as you could with it on. With walkies and a pair of cheap binoculars, you could believe that you were performing reconnaissance on some imaginary battle group.

The car was sometimes used to go down the road to honk for the wayward wanderers who might be in the forest or the fields.

The toughest communication was to connect between the cottage and those out touring or fishing in the motor boat or on the canoe. The only way we could do this apart from standing on the beach hoping someone would see you wave was to put a bright towel hanging in the trees as a sign to come on back.

As with any place that you truly enjoy being, you never really wanted to come in from your play at the beach or on the road. So more often than we would like to admit to our kids, we would find that the incoming messages were scrambled and that is why we never came back up. However, mothers and grandmothers could always rely on rumblings in the tummies of active children to make them return to base eventually with the perennial question, "What's there to eat?"

30. I Know a Secret

I always enjoyed social studies in elementary school. (Well done, great teachers!) The many stories of explorers fascinated me. Perhaps the combination of historical context and geography made it interesting. But I suspect it was the personal adventure that the explorers represented that was inspiring. They endured the unknowns, the hardships and sometimes the successes. This was great stuff for young people to imagine along with their storytellers.

The cottage was for us the ultimate place to explore. The woods were seemingly endless and varied. The rocks provided instant forts and hideouts. The ferns offered wonderful camouflage to see but not be seen. So much to see and enjoy.

Mary Lake with its streams and rivers provided a different kind of adventure. You could explore the coastline of the lake and see various kinds of native inhabitants. Some were in deep meditation. Others were trying to catch their food with various fishing poles. Local inhabitants could be noticed moving in the water. Some parts of the shoreline were just bush. Others parts hid dwellings far up in the woods. This could be any place or time you wished to imagine.

For us, we had a special place that we would try to visit regularly over the time each summer. It meant taking the motor boat across the lake until we were near a series of cabins at the mouth of a river. Like Victorian explorers Livingston and Stanley, we would explore this mysterious river.

As we entered the river, we would slow the motor boat down to a put-put. Not long on the river, we could feel the temperature of the water warming through the aluminum boat. On either side were some small cottages with docks. The width of the channel was large enough for a couple of boats to pass each other comfortably. As we followed the river upstream, we would see a variety of birds including a reliable kingfisher that would remain quite visible on a wire or tree nearby. Continuing further, we would then encounter a large log that was well established to the south side of the river. Usually a small flag was planted by person or persons unknown on that log. Sometimes it was a Scottish national flag; sometimes it was a pirate's flag.

Before long, we came to the first bridge. Due to the water levels, these bridges required all aboard to duck. If the water was particularly high, you had to lie flat in the boat for a successful passage up the river. Looking up at the underside of the bridge, you often saw small bird's nests that had been built there. If the birds were still nesting, they were not amused at your adventure under the bridge and would squawk at you to be sure you did not do this next time.

Immediately after the first bridge was a startling discovery. On the north side in the tall bulrushes was a pair of overalls and rubber boots sticking up in the air with the rest of the poor farmer submerged underwater. What was it about the northern air that brought out a keen sense of humour?

Lily pads with their white lilies in bloom would begin to cover the edges of the shores. The river would then begin to meander more so that you could no longer see very far ahead. Either side soon showed tall grasses with some bushes hanging over the water's edge. It began to look more like Florida's everglades than a northern lake. You could begin to see breaks in the grasses where some kind of creature had slid down into the water. We would imagine alligators although parents would try to assure us that they were beavers, otters or muskrats. More turns and you might see a turtle swimming or sunning on the shore. If you were very quiet, the Great Blue Heron might be on a fishing expedition around the next bend.

Finally, our "secret river" would open up to a small lake. There we could explore the edges with its bulrushes and water plants. The center was shallow and open. One of our adventures with the kids was to go in circles with our little boat. They would giggle at the front as we spun around. We would see the small engine churning the water like a hand blender. We would joke that we were creating Jell-O. The waves we were making gently floated off into the distance. We could try to explore the small tributaries that fed into the tiny lake. In our imagination, we really were like Stanley and Livingston, looking for the source of our secret river.

31. Not for the Faint of Heart

The cottage road was central to many of our experiences. It brought together so many of our memories. It was our arrival. It was our departure. It was our escape during the day. It was our curiosity in the night. It was our terror in the absolute darkness. It was both an old friend and an adversary at the same time. It was a mystery.

In our youth, we were allowed to sit on the hood and sides of the grand old cars as we made our way up the cottage road. This was great fun as we would bounce along feeling ferns and occasional branches whisk by us and over. In later years when hoods were too fragile or too short to sit on but before airbags were introduced, one of the little kids would sit on the driver's lap and steer the slowly moving car down the cottage road. Once we had a van, the new game was to open the side door and "ride Army" with the wind blowing through the vehicle.

The road was a great place for dogs. Throughout my life, we have enjoyed a variety of canines in the family. One word that the they came to recognize very early was "cottage". All of them loved going to the cottage and upon arrival at the end of the road, we would open the car door and release them to begin their run. Regardless of their age and stage of health, each one found new energy to race down the road. It was hard to keep up with them. The most intelligent dogs bypassed the cottage. They kept running down the many stairs to the lake to cool off. My childhood dogs were Treavey the cocker spaniel, Heidi the mix whose digging of Mom's rose bushes meant that she went to the farm (which we hope did not mean that she bought the farm!) Then came Spooky the talented "Heinz 57" dog who could smile on command and who was with us for most of 15 years. After college it was Muffin who lived a long time followed years later by Muffin 2.0 who we parted with in 2010 after 14 years. Tucker the English Border Collie/Australian shepherd mix was the first dog that we included while still having the old dog – in this case Muffin 2.0 After Muffin 2.0 was gone, we have added Shadow who was supposed to be another English Border Collie but turned out to be more German and Aussie Shepherd. Alas, our newest dog Shadow – the hound/shepherd mix – never knew the cottage. These four-legged friends have been etched on our hearts and lives over their years of companionship. No place more enjoyable to have a dog than the cottage where they could run, swim and walk with adults and kids alike.

At dusk or dawn, we often would be driving very slowly trying to come upon one of the many animals who might be proceeding down or across the cottage road. Many a fox, porcupine, deer and rabbit could be seen if you timed it right. Once in the headlights, it was a picture that could extend a few seconds to a few minutes as both car and beast sized up the other waiting to see who would move first.

As you know if you have spent any time in the north, there is nothing quite like the darkness of the cottage road. For the seasoned cottager, the darkness brings into focus the myriad of stars and the constellations above so little noticed with the light pollution of the city. Up north, the entire celestial creation was on display to enjoy. You could watch the changing seasons as the constellations moved to different positions on the night canvas. Whether on the road or at the lake, it was a wonder of starlight, the Milky Way and occasionally the aurora borealis dancing to the north.

But for many of the visitors, that darkness is a very different experience. The seven tenths of a mile before you can see light through the woods at the cottage is absolute terror for visitors. After about half of the distance was covered, we would turn off the car and sit in the silent pitch black of the night. You really could hold your hand in front of your face and not see anything. Even the stars and the moon provided little comfort. Anyone with a healthy imagination or memories of The Hobbit could be sure the forest was alive with large creatures crawling closer and closer to their prey us! Some of the most stout-hearted people were very anxious to restart the car. Some were quite concerned about where it was they had agreed to go. The cottage light flickering in the distance never looked so good to the weary traveller now quite sure that they had passed into the great, dark beyond.

The Road possessed many moods and was not to be trifled with if you knew what was good for you. But like all passages, it could just as easily reward you for having the courage to try.

32. Ready – Set – Fire!

One of the ongoing list of chores included preparing the firewood to season for the coming years. As the fireplace heated the cottage, firewood was not just an accent to enjoy. It meant a good night's sleep and a cozy morning when you wanted to take the chill off.

Those who were skilled in making and keeping the fires aflame were highly prized in the family. Those of us who could build a good fire and enjoyed making it felt some real satisfaction when the fire was burning brightly and smoke was wafting out of the chimney. It was a kind of right of passage to be able to set the fire. This usually involved being seen helping the adults with the fire for extended periods to where the convenience of having the son or daughter set and start the fire overcame the fear that they would burn the place down. It rivaled the "You'll shoot your eye out!" parental warnings of pellet and BB gun lore a la "A Christmas Story."

Somewhere along the way, you had to be willing to gather the small sticks from the forest floor that would become the kindling. This was put in the kindling box that always looked like a very complicated version of Pick-Up Sticks. If you were particularly fortunate, you might have some wood pieces left over from a construction project. Later on, these cast-off pieces of wood from two-by-fours and other wood debris were conveniently sold at the gas station in large bags that were mixed into the kindling from the forest.

Some years we would have a dump truck deliver wood from one of the firewood yards. I went with a friend in his dump truck one year to buy some wood from a firewood business in Kearney just north of Huntsville.

I remember the sensation of feeling the dump truck rock as the white pine, spruce, maple and oak piled into the back of the truck. Complete with the requisite checkered flannel shirt, jeans and work boots, I stood there in the drizzle at the top of the pile in the truck shifting it around. I can still remember the intense sweet smell of those varieties of wood mingling in the air on that fall day.

One of the lessons anyone on fireplace duty learned quickly was the importance of the word "seasoned." It was the difference between looking like a fireplace fool and a fireplace genius. The wood that was often delivered was freshly cut. That meant that it was still green with a great deal of moisture still inside. If you could get the fire going it would not be long before that "unseasoned" log would fill the fireplace with thick smoke and the fire would soon give up the fight to burn that log. Firewood that was seasoned (usually after a year) was a better deal. But one of the advantages of a long-term cottage relationship was that you could actually let the wood season two or three years or more. These logs made you a fireplace hero with some secret power over the otherwise reluctant logs.

Another life lesson for the cottage logger was the face cord and the bush cord. A face or rick cord of wood is a pile four feet high by eight feet long with an average length of sixteen inches for each piece. The bush or full cord of wood is four feet wide by four feet high by eight feet long with the average piece again being sixteen inches. That is much more wood to stack – a mistake you will only make once!

One of my joys was to swing the axe on a cool fall day to split the larger logs into smaller pieces that would be easier to use in the beginning stage of your fire. The full logs were best to add just before bed to keep that familiar chill off the cottage for as long as possible. We had a very large, flat stump that was perfect to set up the log for splitting. It was always a measure of the axmen and the wood to see if the split could happen with a single well-aimed stroke. The logging uniform of the un-tucked flannel shirt, jeans and boots were of course required.

Stacking the wood was a true reflection of personality traits. Some piles were neatly ordered with each part of the row of logs consistently placed. Other piles reflected the "pile is a pile" view of organization. Each piece seemed destined to bring three more with it if you pulled too hard.

It was a satisfied feeling to bring together all the ingredients for the fire and to combine them so that there was fire. As the fire grew from the touch of the old wooden matches to some crumpled newspaper to the assorted sticks and kindling and finally to the logs, the fireplace came to life. The room then filled with the charm of the dancing light of the flames and the subtle smells released by the burning logs.

33. One Dark Night

All cottagers worried about invasion in the isolation that makes a cottage charming in the day but worrying at night. One dark night when all were in bed, I awoke to a sense that we were not alone. Given the number of people usually in close proximity in the cottage would not make this much of a revelation.

However, as my senses became more attuned to the night, I was certain that I could hear something moving in the room. I then thought that I saw something. I called out to my parents that there was something in the cottage. After the rude awakening, they told me to go back to sleep. Whether intended or just as a consequence of being in the small space, I could also overhear the rhetorical question from my father to my mother, "What have we raised?"

Being certain that this was not my imagination, I called out again and then turned on the light in the bedroom. Moments later, I saw the intruder. It flew by. There was a bat in the cottage.

It was normal to see them out catching bugs above the trees and over the cottage. We would see them out on the road or down at the water's edge if we were there in the evening. They were appreciated for the mounds of mosquitoes and flies that they ate. Their squeaks in the night were much better than the jarring zaps of the bug zappers that were in vogue for a while with the crackling sounds of moths suffering the punishment intended for the mosquitoes and other unwelcome types.

The bat was not that large compared to the bats you would see on the old black and white Dracula movies. But this bat moved deftly back and forth. Having seen the bat – I announced that the intruder was real. Finally, the parents and siblings resigned themselves to an interrupted night's sleep.

We can only imagine what that poor bat thought as he saw this collection of three teens and two parents now searching around the cottage to find him. The next ten minutes foreshadowed a scene the movie featuring John Candy and Dan Aykroyd in The Great Outdoors. We grabbed whatever hats we could find including the classic bug hats that covered head and face. A broom was found and one of the siblings found the fishing net. The chase was on trying to capture the bat as it zigzagged through the melee.

Dad being as respectful of other life forms as any member of the Enterprise in Star Trek's The Next Generation insisted that no harm must come to the bat. As he was wont to say about any of the creatures, "He did not choose to be a (fill in the blank here) and he has a family." This Fairley Doctrine of War did not extend to conflicts with biting insects where the application of decisive and overwhelming force was to be used as long as they enemy was not squished on a white ceiling tile!

Clearly, the bat was about as unhappy to be in the cottage as we were to be dancing around the room at two in the morning. It was time for him to take evasive measures by disappearing. Suddenly out of our view, we began a grid search of the last sight in the kitchen area. Slowly we looked around at every nook and cranny. After a time, my brother spotted him nestled between two mugs on a shelf. The bat was so tiny that only the fact that he was a dark spot on a light coloured wood finally gave him away.

Unlike a stray bird that might be safely downed by a tea towel, we had to be more inventive to safely capture the frightened creature. Someone grabbed a discarded can of mushroom soup. Slowly, the can slid forward over the bat. The opening now against the wall was covered with a fly swatter. One of the team opened the back door while the bat can was carried out. Released into the night air, bat and cottagers were all relieved.

We wondered whether the bat would develop a taste for mushroom soup.

We were sure he did not develop a taste for being inside cottages.

34. Shaboo

The cottage was a great center of festivities for family and friends. Whether it was birthdays, anniversaries, holidays or just the joys of being together, the cottage was a place to celebrate. With enough people in your family – and with traditional summer wedding anniversary dates – you could find many cottage occasions that could easily be transformed into a shaboo.

You may not be familiar with the term "shaboo" when it comes to parties or other social events. It is a word that we created to apply to the wide range of social occasions that might involve my dear mother, Lois. Whether in Windsor, Toronto, the cottage or anywhere else, she epitomized the love of people gathering together. It was not limited to birthdays or other celebrations; she could shaboo (a verb as well as a noun!) with people going through tragedy or loss by bringing them the comfort of a visit complete with food, conversation and empathy. If it was a happy occasion, her selection of foods and events meant that it would be memorable.

Through her church in Windsor, my mother along with similar women fed the hungry (and the well fed), comforted the grieving and added their pizzazz to showers, weddings and other fetes. They were a remarkable generation of like-minded talented women.

Never satisfied with a traditional birthday cake, we grew up with cakes made into ships (complete with lifesavers for portholes), moonscapes (with rockets and astronauts landed on it), soccer fields (with nets, balls and players) and anything else she could imagine. Some cakes were in the shape of Mickey Mouse using crumbled cookies for the decorating and large round chocolate ears protruding from the icing. We grew up searching our cakes for foil wrapped coins of all denominations that were baked into them.

So when people were coming or going at the cottage, Mom was always planning the menu to make it special. She loved to take over desserts to cottage neighbours or to church events while there. Mom loved to make jams at the cottage as well. A couple of special boxes were kept there full of birthday, anniversary and particularly Thanksgiving decorations to make the events special for all who were there.

Some of us learned to help by specializing. For me this meant becoming a BBQ expert. While I never arrived at the expert level, cottage life suited keeping the inside stove off and the BBQ on during a hot summer day. So it was a great skill-set to develop. Fortunately, I had some expert coaching from Uncle George Meuser and cottage neighbour Tom Laurie – both people could make any BBQ produce memorable and delectable fare.

As is characteristic of those who love to serve others, my mother the nurse did not enjoy being the center of attention. She much preferred to be in the background seeing others enjoy their times. It was always a bonus for us when we could celebrate her July 6 birthdays at the cottage. In addition to the dinner, cake and candles that the grandchildren would help blow out, we had another tradition. Much to her chagrin, we would turn on a CD with a fully orchestrated and powerful rendition of God Save The Queen. With the volume high enough to compete with the church bells across the lake, we would sing out our version of happy birthday for her. She forgave us eventually. Such were the nature of shaboos at the cottage.

35. The Man in the Green Can

I believe that the early and varied experiences that people have in a place like Muskoka shape a person's view of nature and our stewardship of our world. This is especially true for those who experience the contrast of spending time in a place like Muskoka for a vacation and then return to the overcrowded and industrialized world of the big city. There is something about being in a place where the air is clear and the forests are close that make you have a heightened awareness of our impact on our world. No nature film or green appeal can match the experience of being in such a special place.

In the early days of cottage life, you are very aware of the impact that you had on your environment because most of the consequences of our actions were highly visible and long lasting. Everything was not neatly carted away by garbage trucks to some unknown destination a few miles across town or many hours down the highway to another community or even country.

You would never think of littering on the cottage road. That would be something you would never do because you would drive by that piece of litter again and again. You would not pour chemicals on the land that could seep into your well. You would not foul the beach or pollute the water because that is where you swim. You had no tolerance for those who would damage the environment around you with inadequate septic systems or unsafe practices. Over time, you even developed the sensitivity of how the building impacts the land and forest around you. It would be painful to watch new cottages being built that scraped the natural cover of trees away in order to have large green lawns primed with chemicals.

In our age where "green" usually is "guilt-edged", perhaps it is useful to think back to what motivated people to be sensitive to their environment before green was green. It was the positive view that our role in the natural world was as temporary stewards. The world around us was a gift to be enjoyed and preserved for others to share today, tomorrow and generations from now. It was in being immersed in nature outside of the concrete world that we learned to respect it. The large forest puts our small selves into perspective. The wide sky with its grand vistas reminds us of our tiny place in creation. The passing seasons announce that time will catch up with us too, some day. Our significance comes in part from being a positive part of the story at a cottage, at the lake, in a park or even in the big city.

I think that the little lessons we learned as children have some of the most lasting effects. One of the features at the cottage was the composting can that stood about three feet tall. It was a large cylinder dug deep into the soil. The can had a lock to prevent the nefarious animals from opening it and creating havoc. However, as children we were told that it was good for us to save the scraps of food that might otherwise go in the garbage and to take them out to the green can. Typical of my mother, she told us that there was a little man in the green can who would eat whatever scraps we put in and who was very grateful that we did this. The can was large enough and dark enough that we quite believed the little man was there. We were told that his diet was quite specific and that there were quite a number of foods we should never put in the can. Coincidentally, only foods that could be composted were allowed.

The added benefit of being the eldest was that I could then take younger brothers with me to visit the man in the green can and create tapping sounds that were attributed to the funnyman who lived there. So those were the early lessons about composting circa 1965. Eco-friendly and great fun all those years ago – who knew?

36. Take a Letter

Being at the cottage meant being far away from life in Windsor with the many family and friends who were there and elsewhere. One of the habits that Grandma instilled in us was to send postcards and to write letters. This seems quite novel in the age of email, Facebook, instant messaging and flat rate phone services. Not so long ago, it was a postcard or letter or if very urgent, a phone call might be made with the dreaded long distance charges.

We would have a list of people to write over the summer at the cottage. It would include grandparents, relatives and friends back home. It was great to be able to use the blue airmail paper if we were sending a note to the family in Scotland. Otherwise, it was assorted letterheads and writing paper.

For special people we would find some fallen birch trees and remove a strip large enough to make a postcard. We would flatten out the piece under a book so it no longer curled. Then we would write our letter on the inside of the bark, address and stamp it. Off to the Port Sydney Post Office to mail the letter and away it went. We always thought that like in the book, Paddle To The Sea, it would fascinate the many people who handled it as it made its way to Windsor or elsewhere.

Another form of writing stock was even more unusual. We would find growing on trees some large protruding half-circle of flat fungus. Pulling this off, you could use a stick to inscribe a note and leave it at Rock Island or Fort Rock (up in the hills above the road opposite Douglas Rock et al) as a secret message for others to find. This was long after Little Orphan Annie's secret messages with her secret decoder ring courtesy of Ovaltine and long before geocaching was popular. Mother advised us that it was not appropriate to put fungus in the mail. We were not so sure but not having stamps of our own, we never tried.

In my youngest days the Clark family ran the Port Sydney Post Office, located a little north of the store on the west side of the street. It was a black wooden building with red trim painted on it. Going to the post office to send or receive postcards and letters was also enjoyable as you entered a post office that was very different from any we would find at home. It was great fun to go to Port to check for mail. "General Delivery for Fairley, Meuser or Cowan please," we would say with varying combinations of fear and confidence depending on the day.

The phone I grew up with at the cottage was more like Petticoat Junction or Green Acres than we would care to admit. The cottages along our side of the lake had a "party line" with different rings signifying who was being called. We were the "two rings" cottage. Others were one ring, one long and one short, and two long and one short. While we never were aware of anyone being the kind of snoops listening in as you would see on old television shows, we had a major problem. Our side of the lake included Camp Mini-Yo-We. That meant lonely campers and lonely parents would be calling the camp to make sure all was well. In truth, it was not really that bad in those days and Camp Mini-Yo-We was a model neighbour (excepting the pigs – but that's another chapter) so we really did not mind too much. However when the "private line" was offered by Bell, it was a "yes" vote all around. When I would miss the cottage sometimes in the off-season, I would dial the cottage number and listen to it ring. It made me feel a little connection to that special place. (I was always relieved that no one answered, as I am not sure what I would have said to the intruder who had found a place to hide. I guess I could have gone over my father's checklist.)

In the world that was our childhood at the cottage, we were very isolated with only distant neighbours to visit from time to time. Communication was more likely with the birds and the creatures of the forest around us. Somehow, we not only survived but also thrived in the simplicity of that quiet world.

37. Courage

Being away from the familiar environments of everyday childhood in the city allowed you to encounter much at the cottage that would test your courage.

For some children, it was those early encounters with the gentle waves on the beach. Sitting there in the red sand, the waves would begin to creep forward and suddenly toes, feet, knees and more would start to feel the water. If you were going to exist at the cottage, these early experiences with sandy bottoms and crystal clear water meant that you would need a positive start. Thankfully, the shallow water enabled small children to explore bit by bit with an easy retreat to the shore if their confidence would fade.

Even the older folks rarely would venture too far beyond clam land. The kind and soft sand had already given way to the mucky bottom and suddenly the orange reflection off the bottom had grown to a dark blue and then black. For people used to swimming in many other parts of Muskoka, this would be quite normal as beaches are somewhat rare in the lakes of the north. Perhaps it was the knowledge of the toothy pike and the very large lake trout that could be caught in the lake that kept people from going that far. Perhaps there was a map that had a line that said, "There Be Dragons – or Pike."

The other time that swimming could take a bit of courage would be at night. It is amazing how the same beach and shallows that were quite fine four hours earlier at sunset suddenly became a place of foreboding. Many a swimmer blamed the cool night air or mosquitoes (real or imagined) for their fear of a night swim.

One of my strangest reactions was snorkeling near Dead Man's Island. I had the opportunity to scuba dive in the Cayman Islands and Mexico so I became interested in seeing what was around these islands that I had known from the surface for so long. Once the snorkel and mask were in place, I pulled myself down under the surface. Unlike the bright and cheerful Caribbean, this water went dark very fast. I decided then and there that whatever might be there deserved to be left in peace.

Sometimes the courage was required for activities at the cottage. Going under the cottage was a task that separated men from boys – and often mothers from boys too. It took special inner fortitude to crawl under the cottage (a dry sandy place) with all the characters that might be crawling or hanging around there. Never a problem for Dad who knew that spiders and other creatures were largely misunderstood and should never be injured or killed because "They have families too."

It could be a test to be alone at the cottage even for a few hours or even if you had company – being out in the tent in front of the cottage took an extra measure of fortitude. Many the child and even young teen began in the tent only to be found on the couch before morning.

As teenagers, we would have the occasional water-balloon war in the forest at night. Responding only to sounds, you were literally shooting in the dark as you ripped a balloon at your opponent. We were never sure but we suspect that we soaked the odd raccoon or porcupine in our fevered response to any sound of movement in the distance. Thankfully, they never tossed anything back.

Whether it was courage or just reckless behaviour not understood at the time, we loved to play lawn darts and horseshoes. In the earlier years, it was metal horseshoes that would go flying through the air from one sandy pit to the other on the north side of the cottage. This was a game where you could compete at most ages and could also improve. Years later, lawn darts were introduced. These could be played anywhere but actually worked better on grass where the darts would stick. Once again, it is now a very dangerous thought to imagine these metal pointed darts flying up and down toward the moveable circle. Probably better that we played croquet. With some imagination, we also played badminton and volleyball usually with a hose for the imaginary net. Many of the badminton birdies ended up on the cottage roof – that part we did not imagine.

Keeping your cool during the intense thunderstorms took a stout heart as you could experience dramatic storms in the area day or night. Whipping across the lake the sudden rain and lightning could produce wild weather and huge thunder rolls. More than once, we had lightning strike near the cottage. Once it struck the large tree beside the deck throwing clumps of sod into the air while splitting the tree. Not for the faint of heart.

You could count on times when the power would be out due to a storm at the cottage or elsewhere. Losing the water was always one immediate consequence, as the pump would no longer run. That made having some stored drinking water a good idea. But the loss of lights in the cottage could be remedied with the charm of the old kerosene lamps with their tall hurricane glass chimneys. Set up strategically throughout the cottage when the power failed, these flickering flames gave us sufficient light to live quite well. The oil lamps also seemed to connect us to the generations who not long before battled the darkness with these old lights.

In the 1970s, we witnessed a tornado develop on the northwest end of Mary Lake on a sunny day then turn into a water spout as it went over the lake only to reform again over Dead Man's Island. There it tore off some of the treetops before continuing over to Camp Mini-Yo-We where thankfully it bounced between the cabins where campers had taken cover before flattening some spots along Muskoka Road 10. Thankfully, there were no serious injuries – but yes, it did sound like a train rushing.

As boys and girls turned into young men and women, they were invited to join my dad on the cottage roof. It was a very flat roof so it was not a major risk compared to most homes; but there was something about standing there on that spot. You felt not only taller but older too.

For those who disliked surprises, we will always have the memory of one of the family washing dishes at the sink while my mischievous father grabbed the scarecrow and hoisted it up to the kitchen window coming face to face. The dishwasher was not amused. We suspect the scarecrow was embarrassed.

Visiting the cottage in the winter in the early years took a great deal of courage as the road in was not cleared. The seven tenths of a mile seemed like a week's trek as you pushed your way through the waist high snow. (Snowshoes were bought after the first winter visit!) There was no one anywhere to help you. No cell phones. No emergency solutions other than crawling back out. The cottage was a cold freezer offering only a shelter from the wind but a very damp shelter until a fire was going. The reward for taking this risk was to be able to stand out on the frozen Mary Lake with only the sound of a slight breeze to hear. Nothing was moving. There were no people or motors. Nothing to break the awesome silence of the moment when you felt like you were the first person to ever see this place. Like scuba diving in Grand Cayman, it remains one of my transcendent experiences.

My mother was startled on a first visit in May one year when she slid open the cutlery drawer in the kitchen. In addition to the flatware, we were face to face with a mother kangaroo mouse. Eye to eye, mom cried out and the mouse lit out. However, the mouse forgot to take her litter of newborns with their eyes still closed laying in some shredded paper towel and newspaper. This led to a four-week program of dropper feeding the mice until they could move on to some other foods. We found that they developed a taste for strawberry jam too. After the mice were becoming more mature than the children caring for them, they were released to the forest under an old log. We would leave small bits of strawberry jam on crackers for the balance of our summer there grateful that they were always gone. Steel wool went into all the cracks around pipes and other access points to ensure we did not have a repeat experience the following year.

38. Far and Wide and Weird

On rainy days or nights in the early days of the cottage, it was fun to turn on the radio. With an even basic radio, you could travel far and wide through the night air to the many "clear channel" stations around the U.S. and Canada.

We could be listening to WJR 760 in Detroit, WBBM 780 in Chicago, WSM 650 in Nashville, WBZ 1030 in Boston and occasionally Charlotte WBT 1110 or St. Louis KMOX 1120. We could usually get Windsor's CKLW – the Big 8, CFRB 1010 in Toronto and often CHUM 1050 in Toronto as well. Whether it was listening in on a baseball game, the news or a local show, it was amazing to imagine yourself listening to life in that city so far away.

Locally, we would only receive the Huntsville AM station CFBK and occasionally CHAY FM 93. The local radio station reflected the community well and as was typical of the smaller stations in those days, it could be quaint and quirky at the same time. One of the strangest shows was the Trading Post. Now we loved visiting the various trading posts located along Highway 11 and especially along Highway 60 toward Dwight and then Algonquin. There was always fascinating native arts and crafts plus usually a tee-pee and headdress to wear for a picture. Great fun and an interesting glimpse into the creativity of the artisans (as well as the Made In Japan "Canadian" souvenirs –back before they were "Made In China.") People would come on the show with all sorts of strange as well as everyday items for sale. It was something they no longer wanted or had replaced in an upgrade and now it was time to sell it. From the vivid and enthusiastic descriptions of old tools, refrigerators, bikes and everything else imaginable, you would be sure that these things were near and dear to the heart of the seller. But as you listened to the items described in detail and then priced you had to begin to think that this was an attempt to have someone come by to pick up their junk and pay them for the privilege. It was all very "nudge, nudge, wink, wink" a la Monty Python. They would leave their phone number, often repeating it three or four times to make certain anyone could call. The show host was always both earnest and supportive of the callers.

It was only after you heard the Items Wanted section of the show that you understood that this was serious. People were looking for exactly the same kind of "dump worthy" stuff. It probably meant that there were still a fair number of Scots in the area who see a dump as an acquisition area rather than a place to say goodbye to discards. Our sheds at the cottage and at home spoke to this heritage we shared with the Trading Posts. At one point, it was said that there were more afghans in our basement than there were in Kabul (though ours were folded in storage containers). This show was for real and was a highlight for us to listen and apparently for many others to make a deal.

We occasionally could receive a channel or two on our television with the rabbit ears. With much adjustment, you might be able to point them just the right way to get CKVR in Barrie or Pulse in North Bay. Usually the signal worked best if the person doing the adjustment kept on holding the rabbit ears in that same awkward position. You soon learned to suggest others make those fine adjustments after experiencing the long stand.

The Pulse News from North Bay also had some unusual stories that you were not likely to hear on a Windsor or Toronto broadcast. One interview was with an individual who was commenting on new rules about catching frogs (for the legs!) in the area. This rugged man stood in front of the camera and with 60s quality screen titles it listed his name and then below it the title "Frogger" It was a clinic on how to catch a bullfrog by putting a piece of red felt on a hook then dangling it in front of the great frog. It would grab the felt and the hook and you would reel him in. He went on to explain the impact of some of the new rules on his business and the frogs. Not being those who dined on frogs legs (although I hear they taste like chicken what does anyone who wants you to try a new dish not compare to chicken?), we sided with the frogs on that story. Another individual on a call in show was complaining of "the itch" that apparently was immediately understood by the health care person. He identified the condition came from swimming in Lake Nipissing too near where the lumber was milled.

All of these things helped to pass the hours – usually rainy ones – when all the board games and books had been exhausted. Like city mouse/ country mouse, we were sure our Detroit/Windsor media would seem just as unusual to them.

39. The Road Less Traveled

While most of our journeys were on our main road, we often would go on a different course. That meant a much longer journey so one of the requirements was a good walking stick. The forest was full of great possibilities. Some liked to use the crooked stick that had the easy handle to grab. Others would choose a staff with the tall straight branch to carry along on the journey. It was always another chance for self-expression or self-inflicted jokes as you muddled along like an old man of eight or a 10-year-old wizard.

At the point where the cottage road meets Muskoka 10, a turn to the south would take you across the stream and start you on your journey to the back acreage of the Jackson's land and the only other neighbor, the Wagner's.

The back road to the Jackson's included a walk by very large open fields covered in tall grass and dotted with many bushes and trees. Beyond the open fields to the north was the forest leading to the stream and the beaver dam. As some of the local roads were developed in the 1960s, some of this land was used to supply sand for making the roads creating wonderful dunes to be explored by adventurous children. The open areas on the back road always made me imagine that we were in the grasslands of Africa with the tall grasses covering a sandy soil below. In spite of our many safaris there, the wildest creatures on the savannah were the three Fairley boys.

As you came closer to the junction for the Wagner and Jackson cottages there was a tall stand of trees that had been planted as part of the golf course with two rows equidistant from each other looking up to some outcropping of rocks that was once a golf tee. Near to that point is where the old golf course cabin existed. The fork in the road gave you the choice of heading into the forest which would take you to the Jackson Falls bridge connecting to what was then the main Jackson Road which connected the old barn cottage and the main Jackson cottage with Muskoka Road 10. The other path led to the back entrance to the Jackson cottage and to the north of that the Wagner cottage.

Nestled down by the lake between the Jackson cottage and the Wagner cottage was the log cabin that was often rented over the years. It has some special significance for us as a family because that is where my parents spent their honeymoon and it was also rented by the family when my mother was young in the 40s. It was a four bedroom wooden building with a large common room and kitchen on the main floor. The bedrooms were up the wooden stairs with two having a western exposure to the lake and the other two facing into the woods on either side. There was a nice red sandy beach – similar to what the family would enjoy in the Cowan property to the north years later. The walks each day for some fresh milk to the Trollop's farm formed part of the daily routine. The farm was not far from the end of the Jackson Road at Muskoka Road 10. It had a beautiful barn with the fieldstone foundation. Over the summer at the old log cabin, many new memories were made for that first generation. Before they knew it, Muskoka had charmed them – and the generations that would follow.

40. Jackson Falls

As little boys, we would drive around to the fork in the road that led to the bridge that traversed the Jackson Falls. We would then trek with our mother along the winding road as we looked for interesting stones on the road or perhaps a large fungus on the tree where we could write our initials with a stick. We finally could begin to hear the sound of the water cascading down the falls through the trees. It was close now.

As the old wooden bridge came into sight, we would pause to look for a patch of wintergreen. We would take one of the leaves and chew it for that familiar flavour. The ritual complete, we walked over to the weathered bridge. It had carried the few cottager cars and the occasional truck over the many years it served there. It was a single lane with a couple of dozen planks crossing the structure. It was a great place to sit and dangle your legs over the side.

Facing the west, you looked down on the beautiful falls. Depending on the time of year and the amount of rainfall, you may see the area covered in fast flowing white water as it bounced off the rocks on its way to the winding pool and river below. During the height of the summer, those same rocks might be bare allowing you to climb down and walk beside the quiet water flowing over the rocks. There were many different levels to climb with some being six feet or more to drop. Over time, we discovered the best places for handholds and drop points to land on our way up or down the exposed granite rock. This was one of the places where you learned to connect the colour green with slippery rocks, as you would encounter moss or other weedy growth that might be living on the edge of the water.

If you made it to the fern covered sandy bank of the river, you could have a great adventure sneaking up on a happy frog convention that always took place on the edge of the river. Each frog would plunk into the water and play its game of hide and seek. If you watched closely, you could see them make their way in the water back toward the edge of the bank while still submerged safely out of reach of curious boys.

Sometimes the pool at the bottom of the falls had some natural foam that would accumulate on top of the tea coloured water. It looked like a mocha cream floating on top of the surface that would ride along the river as it meandered over fallen logs and under overhanging pines on its slow journey to Mary Lake.

Looking upstream to the east, you saw the large pools of water that seemed not to move at all even as the water surrendered at the bridge to the waterfalls below. As Winnie The Pooh and Christopher Robin understood, this was a perfect place to race a leaf, a stick or pinecone against whatever your sibling would care to use. It was a game that Christopher Robin et al called Pooh-sticks. Like so many life experiences in the presence of nature, we learned how things move, float and sink as they travel along the currents of a small river. We would launch our fleet and then watch them start their journey. Once they rounded the final curve of the river, we would dash to the bridge to watch them approach. One of the most intense moments was switching to the falls side of the bridge to see if your ship had made it through the hidden water. If it made it then it was over the falls. Your trained eye would follow the stick as it cascaded down with the gushing water pulling it under only to have it reappear further down the falls.

The falls with their ever-changing flow and sounds invited us to visit often. No matter what the season or time of day, we were never disappointed.

41. Half a Mile to Halvastraw

Among the original neighbours were the charming Beth and Ben Jackson. Ben seemed ancient character to us as little boys. He loved good conversation, stories and especially poetry. This was back in the time when poetry was more popular than it is today and the recitation of a poem was part of the social experience. It was like so many forms of oral tradition a part of passing something on to the next generation. There walking through the meadows and rocks or sometimes sitting by their big cottage or on the dock, we would hear him tell his poems. This Gandalf-like figure who was then in his 80s could blow smoke rings with his pipe, would enjoy reciting and then have us recite the poems back to him. As a boy of five or six, I enjoyed the challenge. One of the poems that caught my fancy as a child was Half A Mile To Halvastraw.* Now, nearly 50 years later, I still can hear him say it.

> Half a mile to Halvastraw
> There lived a half-wit fellow.
> Half his house was brick and red
> Half was wood and yellow.
> Half the town knew half his name
> And half new how to spell it.
> If you can wait a half an hour
> I've half a mind to tell it.

*I have never seen this poem in print so my spelling of Halvastraw is a guess.

42. Clean as a Whistle

Just upstream from the Jackson Falls were a couple of pools of water surrounded by outcrops of rock and some sand. This was a perfect place for young boys to go fishing. My mother who was very imaginative spoke of a old fish living there called "Clean As A Whistle". This fish was able to take whatever bait you put on your hook and needed without you being able to catch it. Anyone who has ever fished knows the value of tall tales as a way to endure the uncertainties of fishing. It is especially useful when small children are involved who have neither the patience nor experience to last long without a fish.

In truth, this area typically only had small chub on offer. The nice thing about chub is that they are quite willing to nibble on anything at all, regardless of how sophisticated or unlikely the bait may be. This was helpful for a family on a budget wishing to have some fun. Our bait could include old pieces of bread, fat off some meat or best of all, the ubiquitous grasshopper.

In the open grasslands on our way from the cottage along the back roads of the Jackson properties, we could find many flying grasshoppers to entertain us. We developed great dexterity and skills of anticipation as we learned how to estimate where the grasshoppers would fly and then capture them when they finally landed. With both hands cupped over it, we would carefully grab the grasshopper by the wings and put it into one of our ultra-modern, state-of-the-art grasshopper containers. As may have been true for you too, these were usually old jars with holes punched in the lid. In later years as plastic containers became more common, often an old margarine tub was used. After you got used to the fact that these grasshoppers were highly skilled in the battlefield tactics of how to evade and escape, you were no longer discouraged when so many got away. It made a successful capture even more significant. It was an adjustment for you to get used to the grasshoppers spit which we referred to as tobacco juice due to its deep brown color.

A good supply of grasshoppers meant a great time visiting "Clean As A Whistle." We would use tiny hooks and attach the grasshopper so that it could continue swimming on the surface. This would attract one or more chub that like their piranha relations were just as happy to nibble away at whatever bait was offered as to try a grab and run method. Extra entertainment was had if we included the classic red and white bobbers in the quest. Watching them bob up and down was great fun.

This activity was a useful life lesson in the joys of doing even when it did not mean getting.

43. A Fine Port

In my earliest memories of Port Sydney – known to the locals just as Port – was the closest village to our cottage. We always looked forward to visiting the Clark's General Store. It had the classic screen door in good weather and the heavy wooden door when times were cooler. You could wander around and see an interesting collection of magazines and newspapers to read. As kids, we would also find our way to the novelty area that included games and other small toys that we would assure our parents could keep us quiet in the car on the drive home and entertained in the meantime.

For many years at the side of the Clark's General Store, a pet raccoon lived in a cage. He was quite a celebrity in the village as well is being alliterative. Being Lake People, we had good access to the clams that lived in clam land just beyond our swimming area. If we were going to Port, we would always collect some of these delicacies to offer to our friend Ricky. We would only need to put the clam near the mesh and he was able to quickly secure it and prepare for his feast. We learned from the Clarks that Ricky not only enjoyed clams but was also licorice. So part of our visit to the store included a couple of extra pieces of licorice – usually red – for the raccoon. He was always enthusiastic to grab the end of the licorice and quickly pull it in to his cage. It seems odd now but at the time we never worried about which color licorice we gave Ricky. However, it must not have been too dramatic for Ricky lived many, many years. Later on, the store was sold to the Zanetti family who has continued many of these fine traditions as well as adding some new features including local art and crafts.

Up the road at the north end of Port Sydney across from the town dock was Milburn's General Store. It had the benefit of being close to the public swimming area as well as the town dock where many boaters tied up when visiting Port. Mr. Milburn was a gregarious person who always entertained his customers. Eventually the Milburn's General Store also included the post office.

The Cheese Dock located on the river where the cheese factory used to be was a favourite spot to do some dock fishing. You could find some sunfish, rock bass and occasional perch waiting to meet you. It was a very quiet spot that doubled as a place to tie up your boat if you were doing a quick visit to Zanetti's for some milk or a treat.

At the top of that street was a house that once was the home of a mini-golf course. The three boys could imagine themselves as Arnold Palmer, Jack Nicklaus or Billy Casper trying to win it all, long before there was a Deerhurst or Grandview to test your skills.

A little diner now known as Mary's Lakeside Grill served some fast foods. Finer dining awaited you at the Stevenson's Tea Room across old Highway 11 or you could enjoy the Pump and Barrel across from the Esso. Later there was Smitty's at the Petro-Canada gas station. Perhaps the most notable addition to cuisine in the area came in the 90s called the Beauideal Restaurant that served decidedly upscale dinners.

The Port Sydney public beach was one of the centers of activity during the warmer days. We always sympathized with those taking swimming lessons on a chilly morning when the wind was blowing.

There were some picturesque churches in the area as well. Especially important was Christ Church Anglican whose chimes could be heard playing across the lake when the breeze was right. This grand old church suffered a tragic fire in 2001 but has been rebuilt. The other church in town was the Knox United Church with its classic white exterior and the green trim.

At the community center was a variety of special events including the showing of movies when we were smaller. The one regular event seemed to be Bingo with its unique sign hung out inviting one and all.

Eventually the corridor along Highway 11 and South Mary Lake Road developed with many new businesses opening. We spent a good deal of time visiting Dean's Hardware – always a reliable place to go for whatever challenges the old cottage presented. The Food Town store provided a larger selection of foods that saved a trip to Bracebridge or Huntsville. We visited Paul's Outfitting for any of our sporting needs.

As was true of most of the Lake People, our times in Port usually coincided with bad weather or diminishing food supplies. But for us, it was a fine port!

44. Nothing to Fear – Maybe

In the earliest days of our cottage life, we were very isolated. The only cottage on our long seven-tenths of a mile road was our cottage. You had to travel a good ten to fifteen minutes walking in the water to get to the next cottage, the Wagner's to the south. Further beyond was the Jackson's cottage. In the other direction, it would take you a very long time by water or by road to walk to Camp Mini-Yo-We, our neighbours to the north. Unlike the cottage lakefronts of many areas where cottages were nearly as close together as houses in a town, we were a long way from our neighbours. (Even today, Mary Lake remains one of those lakes with higher lake frontage required, effectively creating more space between cottages.)

For the most part, this isolation was part of the charm of the early years. While the cottage property per se was about half an acre, we had available to us a huge tract of land extending back to Muskoka Road 10 to the Camp Mini-Yo-We property on the one side and the Jackson Road on the south. It was always more likely that you would meet a bear than another person as you wandered the trails through the forests surrounding us.

We had grown up in the hustle and bustle of the city with its many ambient noises. The cottage by contrast was a very quiet place. The noises you might hear could often be angry expressions of nature with its violent thunderstorms, howling winds or strange creatures.

Most alarming was the sight of headlights coming down the cottage road late at night. These could be seen for quite a distance and the sound of a car's approach could keep the imagination running on high gear. Who were they? Why were they here? What were they going to do?

We are not sure who among us started it – or whether it is a primal fear floating in the sub-conscious of the species – but we lived with the image of escaped prisoners approaching the cabin. As children, we had all seen the wonderful B movies featured in Windsor and Detroit on Bill Kennedy's "At the Movies" and the need for escaped criminals to find a deserted area to hide out. We knew that a remote cabin or cottage would be perfect. Were we next? Whether my father shared our apprehensions or perhaps to allay our fears, he always kept a substantial wooden club behind the door that we called "El Cabong."

Cottage windows were also to be feared. The absolute darkness of those nights with no other cottages around meant that looking out a window you could see nothing. So any noises of branches snapping or shuffling sounds through the open screen on the window had us sneaking along the floor to slide the glass on the window shut without making any noise to give us away. The curtains could be closed in the main room but the wide-open windows facing out to the lake were uncovered. It was great to enjoy the view of the lake during the day but for 8 year olds with vivid imaginations. Any number of boogey men or escaped prisoners could be lurking there and looking in at us.

The stray cars ended up usually being someone who took the wrong road as so many of these little exits off Muskoka Road 10 were poorly marked. Occasionally it was a family member or friend who got away from work sooner than expected and came up at night rather than the following morning.

As we got older, we reassured ourselves that our fears were exaggerated. That was until in the early 90s we began to hear about prisoners walking away from the nearby Beaver Creek medium security just down the road toward Gravenhurst. Maybe that wood behind the door was not such a bad idea after all!

45. Creative Licence

It is nothing new to consider surroundings influence a person's creative processes. Whether it is writing, painting, sketching, music or some other art form, where you are can have a great effect to stimulate your creativity or stifle it.

For us, the cottage was a place where the freedom from the everyday routines gave you the liberty to have your soul exhale and then breathe in the wonder and beauty of the place. For me, it was always an easy place to write and create.

For Cari, the cottage not only provided the inspiration for painting and crafts – it sometimes provided the medium as well. She – like so many who have gone to Muskoka was intrigued with the wonderful driftwood that could be found on shore or in the shallows. She could look at a stick or branch, visualize a bird or animal in its shape, and then paint it to life. Her artwork sold well and won many awards as a unique expression of Muskoka life.

For others, the cottage was a place to knit, crochet, petit point and folk art. My mother enjoyed many arts and crafts including eggery. One of her projects was doing copper tooling and she did a wonderful embossing of the cottage.

The cottage was also a great place to enjoy the arts. It was a great place to catch up on overlooked books or books that had become old friends waiting to be re-read. For me, I particularly enjoyed reading the wide range of J. R. R. Tolkien books. In addition to The Hobbit and The Lord of the Rings trilogy, I enjoyed reading all the unfinished tales that would come out from time to time. Perhaps it was that the cottage at times seemed like a place where the wood elves would dwell or that you would not be surprised to round a corner and meet a ranger on the road. We are quite sure there must have been a hobbit settlement nearby but they are difficult to find.

Little wonder that one of the names mounted on the cottage was Loth Lorien. It was a place where there was no time there – it was magically protected from the impact of the larger world.

Another name on the cottage was Langbank – connecting to the historical Wood family farm near Oil Springs, Ontario run by my great grandmother's family and named by one of these relatives the first postmaster at the Langbank Post Office, James Wood after his home town in Scotland.

Muskoka is full of wonderful artisans who capture so much of the beauty of the area. One of our family favourites was William Kratzer. This delightful oil painter had a special gift of capturing not only the beauty of birds and animals but also the rugged terrains of Muskoka. We especially enjoyed the way he used light to bring alive the silver birches in his paintings. We always enjoyed a visit with him in his studio barn located off Highway 60 not far from Dwight. Not only did his art fit the cottage – but also if you took it to the city, it was a wonderful reminder of cottage life.

We also enjoyed the work of James Lumbers. You may know him as the artist who creates works that show a present day scene with some ghostly figures and images of what might have been going on at that place generations before. His work ranged far and wide but some of his pieces included Muskoka. The Lonesome Pine painting pictured a closed Esso gas station that was located north of Bracebridge on Lone Pine Road – something we passed when we would take an alternate route to town. By the way, for those of you (like us) who grew up enjoying televisions The Friendly Giant on CBC and PBS, Bob Homme who created the show and starred as Friendly was the grandfather figure fishing or resting often used in Lumber's paintings.

Whether it was on the beach, on a cliff, on the deck of the cottage or in a meadow, it did not take much to have the spirit within well up and enjoy the creation we were given to enjoy. With all the beauty around us – how could we not connect with our creative selves – not matter how that creativity was expressed?

46. In To Town

One of the strategies that helped us entertain the children on our travels was to create some familiar landmarks. Bridges are an example of that. On Highway 11 crossing the river near High Falls was what we called "The Busy Bridge" with the heavy traffic. On Muskoka 2 along the back way into Huntsville, the bridge that crossed the North Branch of the Muskoka River was "The Bumpy Bridge" as it was always in poor repair and would shake the car or van as we went over it. The most interesting of the three was "The Buzzy Bridge", the Huntsville bridge across the river at the east end of downtown. Once a lift bridge, it would allow boats to pass through. The construction included the metal grates that were typical of that kind of bridge. The effect of driving over it was to feel the vibration on the floor of your car. From the time I was a boy just able to put my feet on the floor – it was always cool to go over that bridge and feel the buzz.

En route to Huntsville in our younger years was a spring located near the intersection of Muskoka Roads 10 and 2. Coming out of the side of the hill was a large flow of crystal clear water that was captured by your cupped hands and enjoyed on a hot day. Sadly, it was eventually posted as an unsafe drinking source when run off from area septic systems new to the area had leached into the water table.

Huntsville was a place where the stores were fun. Visits to Flotrons or the Village Shop would always enchant wives and daughters. The Christmas Tyme and Wooden Penny stores were favourites to as places to browse and enjoy.

A stop into the Louis II Restaurant as you climbed the hill would give you a quick breakfast or lunch where the kids could be themselves. You felt like you were walking back in time there with the sights and smells. The Family Restaurant and Pizza was a good place for dinner together. Part of the 50s and onward was the fast food and ice cream place called Tasty Creem. They were famous for their specially topped hot dogs with such names as the King Ferdie, Emperor Monty, Kaiser Willie and the King Koko. The condiments would fit the country referenced and images of the dog dressed up in the garb of the country were amusing for young and old alike.

Midnight Madness was among the happy family memories as the stores opened their doors late with great sales. They had bands playing at the town hall and entertainment up and down the main street. There were also Pioneer Days with many special events. Among the most unusual was the giant grid painted on a parking lot off Main Street. There they would get you to "buy a square". Then some poor cow was paraded around until a deposit was made with the winning square being the one so designated by the cow. It was fashionably called, "Cow Plop Bingo."

The main street of Huntsville also included a variety of little curiosity shops, hobby and teashops that would reward you for walking up and down the hill. The Nutty Chocolatier and the Yogs were sure to distract the children enough to prompt a tug on your arm to take a peak inside. It was a big treat to line up for a movie at the top of the street. The Dominion Store downtown still included the rollers for your boxes of groceries to zoom along. Many a bored child was no longer bored when able to push the plastic boxes along the rollers until they disappeared into the darkness ready to meet the cars outside.

My parents enjoyed reading The Huntsville Forester in the off-season. We all enjoyed reading the many news and community articles during the season when we were there. Like so many of the local papers, they captured the times well and connected you with the past too through their reminiscences.

A great overview of Huntsville was at Lions Lookout. We have some pictures from the 50s up there. How much of the area has changed. But no matter what decade, it is still great to look out on the Muskoka Highlands.

It was always a challenge to get from one end of Huntsville to the other on a hot day by car or on foot. The sleepy town of the winter and spring was always alive and bursting at the seams when the tourists came a calling. So the announcement that we were going "in to town" was not so bad – even when you hated to leave the cottage for a minute.

47. Rainy Day People

There were some days at the cottage when you just had to leave. These were often rainy days and not really because of the rain. Rainy days at the cottage could mean enjoying a good book, sleeping in late after a busy day on the lake the day before or a time to do some art. For the kids, it could be an all day game of Risk or Monopoly where the hours would pass by easily.

But there were some rainy days…

It might have been a function of the barometric pressure or the phase of the moon. Something made staying at the cottage with the kids unbearable. They would be tense or irritable. Those quiet moments or happy sounds just were not happening. Time to eject!

The escape could be a drive in search of better weather (usually futile since the area usually suffered the same fate when it came to the weather). It might be a chance to do some shopping or catch up on the groceries. But often it became a trip to the coin laundry.

All the various used towels, shorts, shirts, bathing suits, pants and those socks that could still be found had usually been ignored in favour of the sunshine with the lake and the road offering a much better alternative. But if some believed those rainy days were caused by killing a spider – at the cottage it surely was a sign of way too many dirty clothes. The rain seemed to represent the tipping point – to the laundry you must go.

The older cottages with limited water supplies or smaller septic systems could not handle the demands of doing a family's laundry. This would require the trip to Huntsville or Bracebridge. (One time we even went as far as Kearny to find a coin laundry that was available.)

So we would begin by doing a grid search of the cottage for all the places clothes could hide.

Some laundries had places for the children to hang out. That was very good. Some even offered a snack bar. These were great incentives for the kids to stay calm. One of the Bracebridge laundries was next to the train tracks. Watching for trains is good – even if they are rather rare compared to the Lakeshore GO trains.

The biggest challenge of rainy day laundries was that you were probably sharing too few washers with too many other rainy day people. Some would be the dear folks from town who always washed their clothes at 10 a.m. on Wednesday. Others would be cottagers like yourself who just had to get out like you. You could strike up some interesting conversations with others who were passing the time watching their clothes tumble. It was grand to be with the other rainy day people.

The worst time to be there would be if one of the Camps had just unloaded their sheets or other laundry to be done. At that point, find the nearest bridge, jump enthusiastically into the river with your clothes, and hope that going over the rapids would do the wash for you.

48. Beyond the Sunsets

Sunrise – Sunset. Whether you are sunrise or sunset cottagers depends what exposure your cottage has. It might also have something to do with whether you are a morning person or a night owl too. I was assured that there were many sunrises at the cottage. The few I encountered were for the morning canoe ride or fishing trip that called us to an early start.

Our cottage had a beautiful western exposure that meant we were definitely "sunsetters".

The many stars of the night sky would have its own charms. The sunrise wandered through the trees in the morning as the sun first hunted us with its warming rays. It would be a long time before the sun would climb high enough in the morning sky to see our beach and warm the shallow waters for our swim. We loved the bright sunshine and especially the afternoon where sun, wind and waves brought our lakefront alive.

But the sunsets – now that is where the true treasure was to be found.

If you are the kind of person who loves sunsets, you will understand the rich variety of sunsets that you can experience when you have a great view of the western sky. I have had the opportunity to enjoy magnificent sunsets in many parts of the world. To watch the large burning sun slowly descend into the ocean is magnificent. Some latitudes have a very brief dawn and dusk. The sun appears and disappears with great haste. But in the Muskoka sky, our sun takes a more leisurely stroll as it disappears from view.

Many an afternoon would finish with us looking to the west to say farewell to the departing sun who had befriended us on our many activities throughout the day. It was fitting then to pause to see the sun slowly descend in the sky as it rested from its labours that day.

Whatever the season, the sunset would bring alive the trees and the surrounding bush. The many shades of green in the spring and summer would give way to the oranges, reds and yellows of the autumn as they reflected the dying light. The barren trees of the winter seemed to sense that their hope for spring would be renewed again when the sun would return. Seeing a sunset streaking through a gently falling snow was strangely peaceful.

The many skyscapes would add an infinite combination of sunsets for us to enjoy. The range of colours and hues meant that each sunset was something to notice. Whether we were sitting on the deck, at the beach or inside the cottage – there would come a point where the sun was in our sightlines. We would then be entranced to watch the final few minutes of the sunlight flickering through the birches on the hill of the cottage.

Unlike the sunsets by the Great Lakes, the Caribbean or the oceans – our cottage sunsets would see the great eye slowly disappear behind the shoreline and trees on the other shore.

The lake would share in the celebration of the day past as it reflected the colours of the sky and carried the flickering sun on its gentle waves.

Then the sun would be gone. But the sky to the west would hold on to its fading shades of blue, orange and red as if to reassure us that the sun would return again to warm body and soul.

Beyond the sunset? Little wonder that poets, authors and hymn writers used it as a hopeful foretaste of heaven's welcome.

49. The Other Way

While we usually opted to go in to Huntsville for our town visit, sometimes we would go "the other way". The rewards were worth it as so many of the towns in that direction were both beautiful and full of interesting experiences.

Between Bracebridge and the cottage was High Falls. This little park was situated next to a grand cascade of water from the locks above that would flow over the large rock face into the lake below.

As the kids grew older, it was fun to stop into the go-carts located off Highway 11. A simple track with old tires surrounding the edges was a great place to enjoy some speed and roar of the old go-cart engines. Along Beatrice Town Line was a riding stable that became an enjoyable place for Cari and the equestrian minded children. Riding there and at stables past Huntsville on Highway 60 was always a highlight for everyone involved as they saw Muskoka on horseback.

Bracebridge is also remembered for its fine stores. One of the prettiest sights in the area was the Bracebridge Falls. I especially enjoyed seeing them in winter with their Christmas lights up on the great bridge above the falls. The town's people were always very friendly and welcoming. The Bracebridge Examiner did a super job of capturing the flavour of the area. The glimpse it gave into life in the town made you want to read the entire issue.

It was not difficult to convince the children to go the other way if it included a stop at Santa's Village. Like many of the Muskoka children, we grew up celebrating that Bracebridge was on the 45th Parallel – halfway from the equator to the North Pole. Since 1955, it was a natural place for Santa and Mrs. Claus to spend their summers. We would enjoy our visits on Santa's knee after walking through their house. The rides were all themed to Christmas as well. I especially enjoyed the train that would take us around the property. A great place, it continues to enchant today.

Gravenhurst was a place to see Grandpa Cowan and his wife Mary who moved there upon his retirement. It was less visited by us because of the distance but one of the attractions was Sloan's Restaurant where according to my mother was made the best blueberry pies in the world. The Gravenhurst Banner was a paper I enjoyed reading when we passed through.

The Gravenhurst dock was one of the annual reasons to visit that town. The RMS Segwun had been in service to deliver mail and passengers throughout the region run by The Muskoka Lakes Navigation Company. In 1981, the Segwun was restored. It immediately became a jewel in the area for short trips, dinner and daylong cruises on the connecting lakes. The evening cruises were especially memorable.

A very pretty town is Bala including the beautiful Bala United Church next to the scenic Bala Falls. As a pre-teen, we took the back roads near Bala to visit the Mullers, lifelong family friends who were vacationing there. That was one of my most vivid memories of being car sick as we went up and down the old roads. However the ill feelings were forgotten when we were introduced to the very attractive girl with long blond hair who at my age was staying with them that summer to help with the care of their young children. Sadly, it was our only visit.

Port Carling was a later find for us. It soon became a new favourite destination that Cari and I enjoyed each summer with their beautiful locks and the surrounding water. The shops and people made us wish we were closer to their location.

A must read publication for us in the seventies and beyond was The Muskoka Sun that caught life in Muskoka in a very positive way through its wide range of thoughtful articles on the people, traditions and wonder of the Muskoka District. Cottage copies survived for a couple of years to give visitors and regulars some excellent reading about the area. It was 1988 when Cottage Life magazine arrived on the scene. It has always been a good fit for

Muskoka life while it covers cottaging in so many other places as well.

Windemere, Rosseau, Baysville et al were towns that also contributed to the Muskoka experience.

The reason that Muskoka is such a grand place for so many generations is that there are no "bad areas" of Muskoka. Each town, village and lake awaits your time. They will reward you with memories that can last a lifetime.

50. Put the Worm on Tighter Uncle John

One of my mother's relatives who lived on High Park Avenue in Toronto was Aunt Grace and Uncle John Fitzpatrick. They were very interesting people for a young boy from Windsor to visit. Their home was one of the grand old houses of the era full of wood paneling, antique doors and stained glass windows. Their huge backyard was full of places to run and play including a very old woodpile by which to hide.

Aunt Grace was a colourful character who loved doing and saying unexpected things – great for entertaining young lads. She was a bacteriologist at Connaught Labs – very unusual for women of her generation. Uncle John was one of those classic, tall gentleman types. He always seemed like an older Clark Gable to me with his gray mustache and hair. He would always have a ready smile and a twinkle in his eye. (See more about his interesting career in the Cousins By The Dozens chapter below.)

My mother's cousin Murray also had the original ATV called the Penguin car that in the 1960s was a two-seat vehicle that would drive on land and water. Now that was a cool ride for boys of any age.

Not only did we get to visit with them at High Park, occasionally we were together at their cottage at Cop Bay north of Tea Lake on the Severn River not far from The Big Chute. We would have to meet them at a dock near the road. We would hop into Uncle John's grand boat with the twin 80hp engines to ferry us across to the cottage. As we arrived across the bay, there stood the classic dark brown and red trimmed buildings that included two cabins (one of which was the original cottage) and the big cottage build in the 1950s. It was a special treat to be there because as kids, we could sleep in the cabins while the adults slept in the big house.

The topography was different as it had more outcropping of the Canadian Shield. The water was also tinted with the Severn emerald green in places. One of the surprises I once had there was swimming along in front of the dock there when I suddenly realized I was not alone. There beside me was a water snake comfortably using the Diamond Lane and swimming on by me. I was happy to give way. As a young boy, I befriended many leopard frogs living in the moss around the cabins. (At least I saw it as a friendly relationship looking back; I am not sure the frogs would agree.) One of these frogs came to sleep in the cabin in a jar beside my bed. I wondered and wondered how a frog slept. Did it close its eyes? So once the room was dark, I would turn my flashlight on. What do you know? Every time the light shone on the frog, its eyes were open. (It is probably a good thing that I did not end up in the sciences…) It was happy to hop away upon its release on the dewy moss in the morning.

In addition to the excitement of being in a new place to explore and being with extended family (often with cousins Nancy and Hugh with Uncle Stuart and Aunt Joan Cowan) was the fishing. The Fitzpatricks had a large boathouse complete with wide decking inside which housed their boat. We could sit cross-legged with our fishing lines and bobbers peering down into the water below. Like a great aquarium, you could see fish of all different sizes and shapes swimming around down there. Rock bass, sunfish or small mouth bass cruised the waters below. You baited your hook and dropped it in the water. As you watched it descend, you could see the worm settling into its new location just up from the bottom. With the occasional jerk of the line, you could make your worm dance to entice the passing fish with the gourmet breakfast on offer. Then you could watch as this or that fish would swim closer and closer to your hook. Bobber was bobbing and kids were hopping as the fish found itself on a surprise journey up the depths until it hit the surface. Being a young angler, we were coached by Uncle John and Dad as we tried to make it happen. Our little rhyme was, "Fishy, fishy come on my line. Fishy, fishy I'll make you mine!"

Our inexperience, though, led us to conclude that if the fish cleaned the hook or got off on its way to the deck, it was because the worm was not on tight enough. With all the confidence of intrepid youth, we would ask for a better job of baiting the hook next time from our fishing coaches. So the legendary phrase became, "Put the worm on tighter, Uncle John!" Gracious great-uncle that he was, he would chuckle and say "Sure thing!" and put that worm on a little tighter.

51. Moose Wars

Each summer would include at least one visit to one of Canada's greatest treasures, Algonquin Provincial Park. Regardless of the season or the weather, Algonquin was inviting. It too has undergone many changes over the time we have been visiting. However, for visitors to the park it will always be remembered as a place to explore a wide range of nature's many environments.

I remember the very small original museum that would welcome you on the western end of the park. It was a favourite place to stop. Before entering the museum, they had a pool with a number of painted turtles who were variously diving, crawling or greeting you from a log. Once you entered the museum, you could see a variety of animals and birds. We especially enjoyed some of the interactive features where you could press a button and hear the sound of the animal or bird. They sometimes had a fish tank showing some of the local fish. Next was a theater area to watch a slide show or movie about the park. The new museum is a wonderful place to enjoy some time with not only excellent exhibits but also a great observation deck to look out over a wide area of the park.

At different camping areas, rangers would provide interpretive experiences. Our favourite was the wolf calling. The sound of the ranger howling with the distant reply from a wolf pack was haunting and exciting.

The old logging exhibit was especially fun as you could go on the old "alligator", the William M., that looked like a tug boat stranded in the middle of the forest. In fact it was a steam-powered amphibious tug that would transport and manage the logs being assembled for the trip to the sawmill.

Our favourite trail was the Spruce Bog Boardwalk with its variety of walking surfaces in its open areas as well as the forays into the dark forest. We enjoyed the nearness to the ponds as you trekked through the bog area on the boardwalk. At the end, we enjoyed the climb onto the high rocks overlooking the highway.

Highway 60 within the park was always an area that should have had signs posted to "Brake For Tourists". It was not uncommon to see many cars pulled off to the side of the road in the middle of nowhere. This is because a driver or passenger thought they spotted an animal. Sometimes these were deer or bears but for most people, it was the elusive moose that would trigger the mass hysteria to get that perfect picture.

Of course, there were those embarrassing experiences when the car in front had stopped on the side of the road to allow one of the children to relieve themselves or to throw up. Having such a large and unexpected audience is said to have cured many a carsick child while it has given others a new and amazing capacity to wait until the next washroom.

The moose were seldom on the side of the road. They were usually peaking out from the forest. Sometimes they were below the road in the distance in a meadow, pond or even lake. We were told that the salt used in the winter to assist with winter travel was appealing to the moose early in the season, as they would come to the roadside ponds that had become salient. So if you saw a car or two on the side of the road, it was time to engage the battle. Could you shoot the moose before it escaped? Everything from the Brownie Box Camera to the latest in enhanced digital weaponry was put into service. Shoot that moose!

There were certain rules of engagement to be observed whenever you were involved in moose wars. You must slow down gradually without passing the lead car. Hit the side gravel gently with no skidding to startle the beastie. Exit the car only on the passenger side – it is a busy road. The last one out slowly eased the door shut while making sure never to let it bang. NEVER EVER use your key fob to lock the doors. The confirming sound of the horn is sure to get you demoted. If you happen to hit your alarm on the keys, quickly throw yourself in front of the next logging truck – it is preferable to dying from the dozen death stares you will receive from the disappointed photographers when the moose gallops off.Once you are in position, shoot first and oooh and awww later. Don't worry if Junior does not see the moose.

My wife Cari once engaged in such a battle. The moose was in a slightly wooded area. To get a better picture she ventured further and further into the brush until the combination of sticks and bog gave out beneath her. She cut a wrist and earned some other scrapes on the quest. The scar remains. But she bagged her moose, snapped in an instant on the old camera and now a trophy in the scrapbook. The battle was won that day. But the war continues.

52. An Old Seabreeze

As is so often the case in life, good relationships lead to other good relationships. That was certainly the case with my Aunt Joan and Uncle George. With my father being an only child and most of the Fairley relatives being back in Scotland, it was the Cowan side that provided the extended family experience. The nearest relations were my mother's older sister Joan and the Meuser family in Leamington – about 45 minutes from Windsor. We shared many occasions together as families including birthdays and celebrations around Christmas. Both Uncle George and Aunt Joan had interesting careers in education where they both were vice-principals. The four Meuser cousins all were older than we were. Each went on to successful careers. Peggy became the academic, Jamie the physician, Patty the artist and Gord the custom home designer and developer. As younger boys visiting them, they were all very tolerant of their energized little cousins.

The Meusers were part of the cottage rotation in the early years on Mary Lake. Sometimes we would get to see them as we were arriving and they were leaving or vice versa. We had a special fort down at the second beach where the roots of a large fallen tree provided a great place to climb and hide while watching the waterfront. After a time, the Meusers bought a cottage on the Lake of Bays near South Portage. This led to more visits because if both families were "up", then a visit in either direction was likely over the weeks. It was a great way to keep families in connection while growing up. Later on, they moved to another cottage on Lake of Bays – this time off Seabreeze Road. Many happy memories were made there enjoying chats with Uncle George (a master crossword puzzler) and Aunt Joan as well as times with the cousins. Uncle George would take us fishing or exploring around the many bays that make up this beautiful area. Aunt Joan would always show an interest in each of us as individuals and chat with us about our ideas and our life experiences. This often included encouraging us to have a high view of education and the value of going on to university. Their cottage was on a hill looking down over large grassy area. At the bottom of the hill was a cement shuffleboard. We always enjoyed the great meals made by Aunt Joan that often included some wonderful barbeque by Uncle George. My earliest memories of barbeques were there and Uncle George was always kind enough to teach those wishing to learn.

These connections continued over the generations that followed. My children enjoyed adventures with the children of some of the cousins including venturing across the bay to an island where blueberries could be enjoyed. These larger family gatherings were an important part of creating identity and context for who we were.

The church that Aunt Joan and Uncle George attended was the Seabreeze Community Church a classic pioneer church built in the mid-1890s. Since World War II, services were only held during the summer months including local cottagers up for the season. The old wooden church building faces out toward the bay surrounded by tall old pine trees and an old cemetery. What it did not include was electricity. So before each Sunday service, people like Don Bell would arrive in time to let some of the dampness escape and to light the kerosene lamps that along with the unshuttered windows provided light for the service. An old pump organ dating back to around 1902 would fill the air – especially so when cottager and organist John Emmerson was bringing it to life. The congregation would gather on the old wooden pews following the ringing of the bell each Sunday morning.

A number of the weeks featured visiting speakers or ministers. From my time as a pastor in the early 80s, I was invited by Uncle George to lead one of the services. That became an annual event for me for most of the next twenty years enjoying time with people like Don & Jean Bell, Bill & Barbara Shaw (Bill was one of the founders of IMAX), Cathy & Bob Nystrom, Lyle & Diane Bell, John Robson, Carl and Viola Glos from Windsor and the others who would come to the service.

I have had the opportunity to speak in a wide range of contexts but Seabreeze not only is memorable for the kind people and lovely setting but for the occasional chipmunk who would venture in the back door and listen to the message. It is not clear whether they approved of the topics or not as they were never in line to say farewell with the others after the service. Perhaps the fact that they were there more than once was a good sign.

53. What Do You Mean By "There"?

Having grown up in Windsor with the minimum six-hour drive to the cottage (plus any family visits that my mother was able to convince my father to include along the way) we were very experienced long-haul adventurers. In the early days the trip often included lesser highways before the 400 series was complete. That would often mean traveling through the center of small towns along the way. We came to understand the importance of knowing the difference between 11 and 11 B on the highway signs. That B designation we learned as children was the business district and a much longer trip. So as the roads improved and the highway system expanded more and more of our journey no longer required the slow stop and go of the small towns. At some point in our lives we stopped asking the question that is the bane of all parents when traveling, "Are we there yet?"

Our parents were able to load three boys in the back of the large old cars and head up the highway. I guess that is an example of the power of the reward – in this case getting to the cottage. We endured many threats to life and limb as our parents would try to discipline us from a distance. When the fighting became worse, we eventually would hear the warning, "Don't make me pull this car over to the side of the road or you're going to get it!" Thankfully, that did not have to happen many times. The other classic warning was that this would be the last time we went to the cottage because of the trauma we had caused our parents during the trip.

As an adult and eventually a parent, it was only fitting that I should also endure the joys of the cottage commute. In my case that meant driving from the Toronto area up to the cottage. On the face of it, this would seem to be a much simpler experience since by the time I was a parent the highway system was so much better than what we had endured as children. What had changed however was the volume of traffic heading north on Fridays and returning on Sundays. If we were driving from Windsor to the cottage, we rarely hit rush hour in trial and virtually never were part of a weekend commute. But for those who have made the journey up the 400 to Highway 11 you know how long and treacherous those trips can be. This could make what should have been a two hour journey extend into three or four hours of stop and go misery. For those of you who have traveled with children, you understand the difference between an hour of highway driving force and an hour of stop and go traffic.

The long trips from Windsor were made easier through playing the many games we could invent to pass the time. These often included getting points for farm animals, barns and farmhouses on our side of the road as we traveled. There was always a bonus if we could see one of the old windmills. We would lose all our points if we went past a graveyard. Over the years, we became expert at knowing on which side of the car to sit based on when we were likely to see a graveyard ahead.

It is only as parents ourselves that we begin to understand the trials that our parents endured. How our parents survived the hours and miles is a testament to their patience and endurance. There should be an "Order of Cottagers" that recognizes those who have suffered the experiences of driving kids of any age for six hours up to the cottage!

54. Saluting the Generals

One of the delights of Muskoka and similar areas like Haliburton, the Lake of Bays, the Kawarthas and beyond are the general stores. Thankfully, many of these have kept their remarkable character over the decades. They were always so different from the stores in the city that they made an instant impression on you. It usually began with the door – and that would be a screen door. Pressing down on the latch, you enter yesteryear with the wood floors, old windows and casual lighting. Each step you took would give you a different kind of creak as you walked the paths of generations before. For many years, the general store was the only alternative to taking a long drive into Huntsville or Bracebridge. The best of the general stores were a collection of necessities and oddities. All of the essentials were there as well as food. The kids would immediately find the candy counter.

While each of the candy counters would be slightly different, they would always include windows behind which were a wide range of confectionery treats guaranteed to delight the children and their dentists. Some of the staples at the candy counter were licorice – red and black in the old days and later green, purple and even blue. There was also a wide variety of penny candy back when you could actually purchase something with pennies. No small brown penny candy bag would be complete if it did not include black balls a.k.a. jawbreakers. These wonderful inventions started black and as the various layers were dissolved in your mouth, they changed color to white and sometimes red. If mom and dad were anxious for some peace and quiet, they might invest in a tootsie pop knowing that that would occupy your mouth a little bit longer than some of the other candies on offer. Dad was always able to find either Mackintosh toffee or peanut brittle to help him survive the cottage experience.

Not far from Port Sydney is a small town of Utterson that also had an inviting, classic general store. It had a porch usually full of interesting products for sale. The store had the added benefit of being near the train tracks and the old Utterson train station which was the stop used by anyone taking the train to the cottage. It was a real bonus if you could be at the Utterson General Store at the same time as one of the freight or passenger trains was rounding the turn and blowing its horn.

The most awesome general store in the area was and is the Robinsons General Store in Dorset. It was always a special adventure to go to Dorset either through Huntsville along Highway 60 and then down Highway 35 or the southern route along 118 Highway into the town. The Robinsons General Store was huge when compared to the local stores that were typical of the small villages. To the young boy it seemed to go on forever as you went from room to room each filled with a variety of useful and even necessary items for cottage life. There was always a great array of fishing and hunting equipment as well as hardware and knickknacks. At the very back was a room that contained boots, hats and other clothing. One of our special traditions was to purchase their native made slippers with the rabbit fur lining each year. These warm slippers were a special treat that not only protected against the cold cottage floor but also served as a reminder of cottage life when they were used at home in the winter. We always were delighted to hear that our day would include a visit to Dorset. The drive between Dwight and Dorset in the autumn was always one of the most magnificent you could enjoy. The combination of the flaming colours on the trees with the spectacular rock cuts along the highway was awesome. I have a special affection for Highways 60 and 35 as that is where I learned to drive on the highway in Dad's Grand Ville. Now that was a car! But I digress…

Dorset also had the attraction of the fire tower. If you could (or would) climb the many stairs you were rewarded with a panoramic view of the lakes and trees in all directions of the Lake of Bays. It was enough to want to make you join the ranger service! One special evening was being up the fire tower watching the fireworks from the lake below. What a view! What fun!

As children, we enjoyed our visits to the general store. As parents, we needed the general store for the distraction on a rainy day plus the wonderful supplies we found there. Throughout United States and Canada there are many general stores that remind us of a simpler time when service and relationship was as important as the bottom line.

Hooray for the creaking floors and screen doors of the general stores.

55. The Muskoka Blues

Growing up in the deep southwest of Ontario in Windsor and Essex County, we lived our lives visiting the many roadside stands that would feature wonderful fruit and vegetables local to our region. That meant rich red tomatoes and other great produce that grow so well in the rich clay soils of the area. You could always tell someone from the county by how they referred to cucumbers. They were always "cukes".

Unlike today, blueberries were a special treat reserved for those who could purchase them up north. This was especially true of wild blueberries with their distinctive sweet taste. At the cottage, we had some reliable areas where one could find patches of blueberries waiting to be picked. It was usually into August before the spots were ready. We would take a little container with us to begin the quest. Like everything in Muskoka, you had to compete with the other residents. For most of our cottage years, the other residents were of the four-legged variety. Occasionally it would be a deer or bear but we always suspected that the raccoons and chipmunks were our greatest competition. Somehow, we never minded the fact that some of those bushes had been raided since we all loved the animals as part of the Muskoka story. One of the most interesting connections between beastie and blueberry is the dreaded blackflies. They have apparently hired a public relations firm to help improve their image. It is now rumoured that blackflies are responsible for pollinating blueberry bushes. Now, I have never seen this scientifically verified but it is a great line to use – if you are a blackfly.

We were particularly fortunate on our side of the lake and with our sandy soil to enjoy a wide variety of berries that became available at different times throughout the summer. They range from wild strawberries to wild raspberries to wild blackberries and of course the dreaded chokecherries. Bushes along the road grew heavy with the many raspberries and blackberries. The wild strawberries tended to grow on the north side of the cottage in the sandy patch located there. Those took some extra bending to add to the bucket. The raspberries and blackberries were always at a comfortable picking level.

For those who visited us at the cottage in August, a walk into the meadows to find some chokecherries was part of the experience. These deep red berries hung on trees and were easy to collect. We would tell our visitors that our mother liked to make choke cherry jelly. This was true. It was also true that my mother tended to add a significant amount of sugar to the jelly to make it edible! So it was always a surprise for them to bite down on their first chokecherry and see the strange expression on their face as the very sour and dry berries forced them to pucker up. Ancient legends suggest that the chokecherry was used by socially awkward man who could not think of any other way to encourage their dates to pucker up. We have no first-hand evidence of how well this might work as a strategy. What we can report is that a sustained pucker can be seen on the most reluctant faces.

The few blueberries that we could pick over the season ourselves were never sufficient to make a pie, add blueberries to muffins or to enjoy on cereal for any length of time. So part of the return trip to Windsor in August always included a visit to one of the many roadside stands on Highway 11 southbound. The stands would appear early in August and would last sometimes until Labor Day. Regardless of what other fruits and vegetables they may sell, it was blueberries that always were featured on the sign. Depending on how many or how few dollars were left in the wallet in the age before debit cards and bank machines, you may be able to take home anything from a pint of these blue wonders to a 6 quart basket.

We all enjoyed them for the flavor and the association with Muskoka. We never knew about the powerful antioxidants found in blueberries. Had we known at the time, we might have eaten them anyway. It was always an act of great faith and terror to pull off to one of these roadside stands. The traffic was always coming along at high speeds with winding corners to obscure your vision. But such was the magic of the marvelous blueberries that mom was able to prevail upon dad to risk it all. Like bringing back cheese from Wisconsin, there were always many requests for us to bring back some extra wild blueberries to friends and family. There were many trips that were shared with baskets of blueberries leaving the Canadian Shield on the journey to the land of cukes and tomatoes.

56. A New Age Was upon Us

In the early 1980s as the Jackson family who owned the undeveloped lakefront and back-acreage around the cottage departed the scene, the inevitable changes were about to happen. The remaining lake lots between the Jacksons and Camp Mini-Yo-We were gradually purchased and new neighbours were coming.

It is a truism of most cottage areas that after anyone buys a cottage on a lake, they believe that this should be the end of all development. It was going to be a big adjustment for us to have our pristine (or rugged – depending on your point of view) world changed. We were careful to remind ourselves that we too had been a change for the lake when our cottage was built and the road was established. But we knew that the scale of these developments would dwarf our tiny footprint from the 50s as the nature of the times and the opportunities to build grander cottages in the 80s. Muskoka was now a well-established area with good road access coming up from Toronto. While the big lakes like Lake Muskoka, Lake Joseph and Lake Rosseau had been developed on the one side of Highway 11 and Lake of Bays on the other side, it was no surprise that some of the remaining northern lakes like Mary would be developed.

We were very fortunate in our new neighbours. First to the north of us were Bill and Marion Havercroft, cottagers who were moving to a larger cottage to accommodate their growing extended family. Then Tom & Nancy Laurie arrived and added beautiful landscapes and architecture to the lake. Later it was Jim and Dorothy Copeland who purchased the site overlooking the bay and Camp-Mini-Yo-We where they had long been associated. Toward the end of our time there, another severance created space for Keith and Pam Conklin. Following the sale of the Copeland cottage, we welcomed Grant and Shirley Bartlett as new neighbours.

To the south, the Bradleys came to the Jackson's cottage. The Veals and Bells built on the area where the old log cabin had been and then the Tabbits built a beautiful place on what was the Wagner property across the stream from the Lauries.

The quality of these relationships made the transition to the new reality easy to bear. While we endured years of road upheaval, as the construction of the various cottages was underway as well as the unfamiliar sounds of building, it did come to an end. With the additional neighbours, we had the benefit of a much better road (farewell to the scythe) and some enhancements like a tennis court that one of the neighbours generously shared with the rest. In addition to the contacts at the waterfront or on the road, visits to each other's cottages over the course of the summers built the relationships.

We also had an annual tennis tournament and BBQ dinner that brought together the families from the Bradleys on the one end of the area to the Copeland's at the other end. Mrs. Havercroft and I were the surprise doubles champions one year – a credit to Mrs. Havercroft's excellent tennis game.

It was a new age that changed our world there. As with all ages, they bring their gains and losses. The good people who had become our neighbours made this new age much easier to face.

57. Watching Scotty Grow – and Doug, Beth and Emma Too

Places that you have the opportunity to spend time together as friends or family are where many of the wonder of life happen. Of course, there is the excitement of travel and the marvel of invention. So many things inform and entertain our lives. Education and vocation also can be very exciting.

However, for any of us who have had the privilege of being part of raising children as part of our life story, you understand when I say that it is full of wonder.

Depending on their age and your age, you may wonder why you ever thought being a parent was possible. Depending on their age and stage, your children may agree with your self-doubt.

Yet somehow, through all the uncertainties, confusion, mistakes and terrors in the parenting process you have the privilege of being known as their mom or dad.

Parenting does teach you many things. Whatever supposed expertise you may have from your exposure to child and developmental psychology, education, books, seminars and courses, what you do know for sure is how little you really know. There is nothing quite as humbling as being a mom or dad. That is not a bad thing because as any educator will tell you, knowing that you do not know is the beginning of knowledge and even potentially wisdom. I am grateful to each of my children for all they have taught me about life. It is life-long learning when it comes to being a parent – and that's a good thing.

Cottage life has been a place where you can do some graduate studies with your kids. Being together in such a wide range of experiences for blocks of time is invaluable in getting to know your children and building lifelong connections with each one individually. As it was for our parents, time spent holding a fishing line, looking down at an autumn leaf ablaze in colour, splashing in the lake or canoeing up the river was priceless.

Having a picnic at Rock Island on a sunny day or walking on the road as far as we could go all became part of our shared experience.

Among the best moments were cups of cocoa together after a long day with some cinnamon toast on the side. Grandma would always ensure that some mini-marshmallows were bobbing in the old cocoa mugs.

If we were racing across the lake in our not so speedy motor boat, you might have heard the singing of "Day-O" or other strange tunes being belted out.

A casual observer would wonder at the lack of accuracy in our throwing balls at the lake. To create the famous "athletic dives" at the cottage, we would throw a ball in the lake just out of the normal catching range forcing a spectacular effort to snag the ball.

There was nothing to compare with the classic watermelon shampoo experienced after most of the watermelon was eaten at the beach. With what looked like a watermelon helmet, the remaining rind was applied to someone's head and spun around creating a fine mess. It was quite a sight.

Fishing expeditions to "Clean As A Whistle", the docks or the islands meant that I had a captive audience where I could watch and listen to them talk about their wonders and their world. Between the fishing rods, tackle boxes, nets, oars and containers of bait, it was never dull and rarely quiet. In spite of this we caught fish. One of the strangest catches was a slightly rusty child's fishing rod that had accidently gone into the lake with an overly enthusiastic cast the previous summer. It was fitting that the same angler who made the cast recovered the fishing line. A year older and a great story added to his life.

Many hours were spent playing paddleball at the lake. We enjoyed playing the catch game with the Velcro paddles that snagged the tennis ball – so much easier than a glove!

You can close your eyes and see them toasting marshmallows over the fire.

Nothing was as special as the bedtime stories before tucking them into bed. These all will live on as the best of times for us.

Life at the cottage as with other experiences when time is invested with our children expands the common area of our relationships. We have more memories of good and challenging experiences that bind us together forever.

Parents soon learn that each child is very different in spite of similar DNA and environment. All develop their own identity and unique interests. Some seem to echo their parents but often they seem to be more like a reflection of grandparents or someone in the distant family tree.

One of our favourite family movies, enjoyed many times at the cottage, is the old Cary Grant classic, Arsenic and Old Lace. In the movie, eccentricities and unexpected twists make the comedy very charming. At one point of exasperation, Cary Grant announces, "Insanity does not just run in our family – it practically gallops!" We would concur along with all who are parents.

We are very grateful for each of the unique and wonderful blend of traits, abilities and mystery in each of the children as their life story is being written. I value my memories with each of them. I continue to enjoy the changing relationships as they grow up. All of them are fun to be with as people. That's not a bad starting point. They are all interesting as well. That makes for great conversations.

Cottage time has been an important ingredient in watching Scotty, Emma, Beth and Doug grow. Doug and Beth are now adults (Beth recently enhanced our family through her marriage to Matt.) Emma and Scott are now both in their teenage years. There is still much for us to learn from all of them. We look forward to the continuing education.

58. Blessings Received

When the air turned crisp and the painted forest began to shed her orange, yellow and red leaves you knew that the cottage season was coming to an end. For those of us in Muskoka with the Canadian Thanksgiving coming on the second Monday of October it was always too soon. We always wanted to extend our time just one more weekend but by the time Thanksgiving came, you had often seen a skiff of snow and the change of season was not far off. For the non-winterized cottage, the dread of frozen pipes loomed large in the mind of every father.

While I have enjoyed Thanksgivings in the city and elsewhere, my favourites still are those held at the cottage. It always included the important reminder to be grateful for the many blessings of life we enjoyed in life that for our family included a spiritual celebration at church. Beyond that there were many other traditions bound up in the Thanksgivings at the cottage.

The drives north were never quite as busy on Thanksgiving weekend. Most of the colours in places like Muskoka, Haliburton and the Kawarthas had peaked a week earlier and your weather was unpredictable. The die-hard cottagers were usually the ones who would be heading up the 400 Highway to Highway 11 to put the cottage to sleep.

Depending on the year, we may not have been up to the cottage since Labour Day with the distance of driving from Windsor for a weekend. For my parents, longer annual vacations and later retirement gave them more time to enjoy the autumn season by the lake. For us, being based in Toronto in later years made those fall weekends much more possible. When you could have the extended family together for the day, it was an extra special weekend even with all the closing chores that were required. Come to think of it, having the extended family there was probably a good management decision by the parents to ensure everything was done!

Sometime during the weekend as the sun was breaking through the trees on the road, we would pull out the "cottage football" long ago retired from our more active use at home. It would survive the seasons in the cottage shed with the ice-cracking temperatures in the winter and the intense heat of the hot summer days. Sitting near the fishing tackle and not far from the lawnmower, it accumulated a variety of smells that greeted you whenever you entered the shed. After the old football was pumped up once again, our Thanksgiving Bowl Game would begin. The road suited long or short routes – no need to go wide as the trees provided wonderful coverage. It was a great way to work up an appetite for the turkey dinner – or recover from it!

59. The Turkey and the Church

Churches and community groups in the surrounding towns often had a turkey dinner celebration to gather the community and raise some money.
(We often wondered whether they did not use the proceeds to have another
dinner celebrating the departure of the seasonal visitors with the traffic and
chaos as well as business that they brought each summer.) The two nearest us
were the Port Sydney and Utterson turkey dinners.

The Port Sydney dinners usually coincided with the "Cavalcade of
Colour" events the weekend before Thanksgiving which encouraged visitors
to come to the area to see the fall colours. If you have ever seen the changing colours of the maples and other deciduous trees of Vermont, Michigan,
Minnesota or Quebec, you begin to understand the attraction. The Muskoka
District enjoys some of the most intense autumn colours to blend with the
faithful greens of the fir trees on each hill and around each corner.

The dinners at Port Sydney were held in the large community hall. It
included a long line that wound its way around the grounds. At the front of
the line were the ambitious, the impatient, the famished and the skeptics who
were sure that this would be the year that they would run out of pumpkin pie.
On those years when the rain drizzled down on the waiting crowds, people
felt a little less guilty about enjoying the bounty having survived the damp
and cold. When the weather was kind, the line became a place to visit with
neighbours known and unknown.

Utterson's line would extend from the community center across
from the United Church down past the General Store. Cars were parked in

very creative ways under trees, in fields and on each shoulder of the road that somehow still allowed people and other cars to journey up the hill to the promised land. What was lacking in milk and honey was made up by turkey, stuffing and a wide assortment of pies.

One of the critical decisions for each of these events was whether to be a plate or bowl event. The plate events created an assortment of turkey, vegetables and potatoes served to each person to enjoy. The rolls and butter were waiting for you on the table. The alternative was to do the dinner "family style" with serving bowls and plates ferried to and from each table by the servers. This usually provided for a faster delivery than the controlled portion plates did. But as you would expect, the flexibility of the dishes meant more food was enjoyed at each table. The family style tables also provided some of the funnier moments at these dinners.

One year we were at a very long table that was half our family and half others. Many of our family members are rather substantial (One physician said that our genetics were based on living and starving in the remote highlands of Scotland!) but having been well trained by the various matriarchs of the family, we would enjoy average portions of even a great turkey dinner. In this case, the other end of the table received the full bowls. As they were emptied, they would be picked up by a different server on the other end. We watched as bowl after bowl were delivered to the other end but through some cruel magic, by the time they reached our end of the table, they were empty. The other end of the table was not only ambitious in how much they ate, but were given credit for thoroughness as each bowl that passed beyond them was very empty. Our wonder turned to amusement. It was one of those times when you would expect to see Allan Funt or his successors with Candid Camera to catch your reactions. One dear lady at the end of the table looked like she could account for a great deal of the food that had passed by. Over the course of the meal, we began to receive some bowls that included more and more of the bounty. But it was clear that a significant deposit was made on the lady's plate as each bowl passed by. The desserts and coffee came later with the usual assortment of wonderful apple, cherry, blueberry and pumpkin pies. Our suspicions were confirmed as we watched what appeared to be a slow motion collapse of the lady's plastic chair as all the legs spread out and she found herself having that last piece of pie on the floor. As others rushed to help her up, she was able to salvage and finish her dessert.

If a good laugh aids the digestion, we all digested that wonderful dinner very well indeed.

60. Fond Farewell

There comes a time when aging parents, mobile children, deaths in the family or changing finances cause cottages to be sold. Different from selling a house – and perhaps more like selling a family farm – the sale of the family cottage changes each family in many subtle and predictable ways.

In our case, the worry for my aging father about the tree that might fall on the roof in the winter outweighed the gentle breeze of the summer day or the peaceful sunset shining through the autumn leaves. The travel of six hours from Windsor and the changes in my mom's health meant that it was time to be done.

In our case, the cottage was sold to our neighbours who had a love for the area and a demonstrated desire to protect the back acres that provided such an important context for the cottages on the lake. It was in good hands.

Without the cottage as a focal point for gatherings, it became more difficult to connect with family in the same way. While it is a strain to have family or friends under the same small roof – you developed a different and deeper relationship than you would when visiting their home for a meal. Just as summer camp or a college dorm creates long-term relationships forged with extensive time together, cottage life produces a unique opportunity to build and deepen relationships with those there.

The sale of a cottage also seals in time the memories of that place with all its stories and wonder. Even if you are fortunate enough to have a different cottage at some point, the cottage that was will always hold its unique place in your story. It is where you saw yourself, your children and sometimes grandchildren grow up. So many firsts happen at a cottage because of the times spent there.

It is a wide world full of many opportunities for adventure. A cottage can become the natural place for you to go versus all the other places you might have gone on your vacation. Its siren song called you year after year to be there rather than somewhere else. In the years since the cottage, our travels have included many different places as a family. Is this better or worse? Who knows? It is different. It is what is for now.

What of the future? Will we be like many of our generation who remembers the simpler cottages of the past? Or will some cottage be again in our family's future? Cottage life certainly has changed over the decades that the Cowans, Meusers and Fairleys were part of the Mary Lake story. But that simple wood frame cottage changed us all too. We carry it with us in photographs, stories and relationships forged over the generations who were there.

Cari used her gifted imagination and creativity to assemble shadow boxes that included a container of red sand from the beach with some Mary Lake water sealed in a glass container. Each background included an assembly of plants or other items to remind you of the cottage. They are special keepsakes.

I am grateful for the vision Grandpa Cowan had to purchase and build the cottage. For my parents and the others who kept it going over the years that followed, I also thankful. The times with family and friends have given us the cottage tales that have enriched our lives and helped shaped who we are. We were truly blessed to have that old cottage on Mary Lake, in Muskoka as part of our story. We bid it a fond farewell.

61. Sandy Feet

If your cottage has a sandy beach, you will understand this chapter all too well. Nothing follows you everywhere quite as thoroughly from the cottage as sand. That is unless you are skunked or your newly perfumed dog goes into the cottage and spreads the olfactus horribilus everywhere. But apart from the skunk, it has to be sand that is able to be anywhere and everywhere.

Whenever we as kids would come up from the beach, we had to stand in the basin of water waiting for you at the bottom of the cottage stairs before you went in to change. It was a rule. It was a BIG rule. If you were spied with sandy feet in the cottage, you could be given any number of chores to do. After you immediately went outside to dip your feet in the tub.

Now you would think that this would not be a difficult thing to remember to do. After all, usually water was waiting for you. Or if not, you could easily turn on the hose beside the cottage to add some water. In go your feet – off comes the sand. Easy. But of course when children (read here especially boys) are involved, what should be obvious and what is clearly easy ain't necessarily so.

In the quest for food, all of the simple tasks like washing off the sand or using a towel to dry off before entering (also a very big deal) are just forgotten. The wiring of the brain (or lack thereof) allows the subject to ascend the stairs from the beach to the cottage grounds and then bound up the stairs and into the cottage without hesitation.

Only when the voice of parental reason (and exasperation) is heard asking if you rinsed your feet and dried off would the malfunctioning brain be exposed. There you would be standing with water dripping off your bathing suit and down your legs only to carry the bits of sand still on your feet onto the floor below. Perfect!

It came to the point that the parents would actually place the water container on the bottom step so that you needed to step into the water before climbing the stairs into the cottage. Sadly, this was sometimes hopped over anyway.

The waiting water served not only the practical function of dropping the sand off but it also was a reminder of the day. Early morning after fishing, your tootsies would feel the chill of the bucket of cold water that had been cooling all night. Later in the day, the warming sun would make the water lukewarm so that it was not noticeable at lunchtime. Late in the afternoon and the water would be hot so that you could imagine your wiggling toes enjoying your own version of a cottage hot tub.

Depending on the number of feet dipping in the water, you might have to clean it out most days. The sand would begin to accumulate on the bottom so that even a good effort at removing the sand from your feet might be in vain. Then there were the various blades of grass or other floating debris that would make the process less inviting. On with the hose and the water would be clear again.

In spite of the best efforts, the sand would accumulate in the cottage and everywhere else. Part of this was of course the bathing suits. If you sat in the sand, the sand sat with you. As you left, it hitched a ride. If you were sitting in the shallows enjoying the calm or bobbing in the waves, the sand would find its way into the most unlikely places. It was always amazing how much sand was in your hair – back in the day when there was hair.

These sand transfers would go throughout the cottage, into the suitcases, in the car and eventually home. So it was not uncommon to find some red sand from Mary Lake reminding you in Toronto or Windsor of your past adventures. When I was younger, my pediatrician did the routine inspection of my ear canals – looking for Mickey Mouse and Donald Duck – only to discover some red sand. He asked quizzically, "Where did you go that had red sand? Prince Edward Island?" "No," I replied. "It was Mary Lake in Muskoka." I am not sure if that made my chart or not but I was pleased to think the cottage was there. (Mom was not so pleased and insisted on a more thorough session with the ear swabs!)

All those years trying to get the sand off.

It would be nice to have some of that red sand between my toes tonight – even if it was in the house in Windsor.

62. James Alexander Cowan

The cottage and all of the memories that were to follow in that place were the result of a decision by my grandfather to purchase the land and build it all those years ago.

James Alexander Cowan was born in Shakespeare Ontario on October 27, 1901. He died on September 9, 1978 at Bracebridge, Ontario and is buried in Gravenhurst – not surprisingly in Muskoka. The almost seventy-seven years that were his life was quite an adventure. It came at a time when Toronto and Canada were coming of age. The whole world was changing and he was there for many of the interesting chapters of the period.

He was the eldest child of Presbyterian minister Hugh Cowan and his wife Jean Wood.

Jimmy Cowan or JAC, as he was often known, spent some time at the University of Toronto before moving on to writing at the Toronto Star. Later he became an editor and writer at Star Weekly. His colleagues included Greg Clarke, Morley Callaghan and Gordon Sinclair. It was during those years that he met and worked with another writer at the Star who was to become a life-long friend, Ernest Hemingway. Just prior to the Hemingway's departure for France,

Ernest Hemingway served as best man to my grandfather when he married my grandmother Grace Williams in Toronto on January 12, 1924 at the Hemingway's apartment in the Cedarville Mansions located at 1599 Bathurst Street.

This young and vibrant Toronto was an exciting place to be in those days and the newspaper business was a great center of community life. Toronto in particular and Ontario in general were just beginning to awaken as a place of industry and commerce. Jimmy Cowan went on to write features for the Star. Between 1926 and 1942 he wrote twenty-three feature articles for Canada's Maclean's magazine. His first article there was at the age of 25. He also wrote satire for Esquire Magazine.

His talents led him to the new world of PR as Canada's first Public Relations specialist (or consultant as they called it at the time). He incorporated his public relations company in 1930 called Executive Services Limited that included some of Canada's top writers who were available to execute the communication strategy. He went on to represent and advise a wide range of firms over the years. It was said that he was known for an intuitive sense of what direction and message would be most effective for a client to take. He was what Malcolm Gladwell would call "A Connector" with the ability to maintain a wide circle of business relationships during a time when "who you knew" was even more important than it is today.

He had an early and continuing interest in the energy business. His special focus was on uranium and radium or what would later be generally known as the nuclear power industry. His many travels included visits to Fort McMurray, Great Bear Lake and Great Slave Lake.

He was a personal and corporate advisor to the famous business magnate Cyrus Eaton of C&O Railway now known as CSX. He was very involved in the public relations world of Steeprock Mines and Canada Steamship Lines in Canada too.

An advisor to politicians and political parties in Canada, his work also took him to serve as an occasional personal public relations advisor from 1935 – 1939 to President Franklin D. Roosevelt. His politics in Canada were usually associated with the Liberal Party of Canada.

He represented Rank Films of Great Britain (familiar for their film introductions that featured a man sounding a large gong) as their Director of Public Relations. At the time, Rank Films produced many of the U.K.'s most important films and was home to many of the great British stars of the era. In addition to the Pinewood Studios (think James Bond Movies), Rank also owned the Odeon Cinemas. This led to numerous hours with the many British actors who would come to North America to promote their films. Among the many actors that he assisted were Sir Alec Guinness, Sir Lawrence Olivier, John Mills, Deborah Kerr, Trevor Howard, Jean Simmons, Stewart Granger, Basil Rathbone, Michael Redgrave and Leslie Howard. This added a great deal of colour to life on 336 Douglas Drive in Rosedale where my mother and the family grew up.

In 1952, James A. Cowan was elected the first president of the Canadian Film Institute (previously known as the National Film Society) by the board of directors.

Over the years, he acquired the rights to the Madame Tussaud Waxworks for Canada and he was the one who brought it to Niagara Falls.

JAC was someone who maintained a range of interests and causes. He wrote a script for a documentary on the discoveries of radium at Great Slave Lake and the development of the nuclear industry in Canada. The film was called The Secret Years of El Dorado that won the award for the Non-Dramatic Script for the 1968 Canadian Film Awards (now known as the Genie Awards).

In the early 1950s, he was one of the founders of the Stratford Festival in Stratford, Ontario assisting with the promotion of the festival as well as the connection to British actors from the Rank Organization who would headline at the Festival like Sir Alec Guinness and Irene Worth as well as the first director Dr. Tyrone Guthrie. He then oversaw and financed the initial PR and fund raising efforts of the project. The day to day work was done by the talented Mary Jolliffe who was the festival's first publicist. Through his connections in Great Britain and the United States media, he was able to have the Stratford launch featured in the international press. It was his concept to promote the new Festival in the same way you would a new movie. His efforts led to excellent coverage by the U.S. and U.K. media. He arranged the documentary of the National Film Board on the creation of the festival called, "The Stratford Adventure."

He was the Canadian Cancer Society's first National Campaign Chairman and helped pioneer the organization serving as a member of the National Board for 18 years.

His love of nature included a number of conservation projects including his work helping to secure Canadian support of the Quetico-Superior Foundation to preserve the boundary waters area that created the largest international wilderness preserve in the world.

In the 1950s, he was an advocate of blended income housing rather than common income patterns in the redevelopment of the then Regent Park slums in Toronto. This was rejected at the time; however, his view proved to be the solution now generally adopted in urban planning in Ontario.

He served on various corporate boards including the founding board of CTV.

Expo '67 was one of his last major projects before his retirement; although he remained involved in corporate life into his seventies.

James A Cowan was, as one writer described him, the "acknowledged master mind of the public-relations business" at age 44. At age 60, another article headlined that he was the "Dean of Canada's PR Men." The article noted that, "When Cowan picks up that telephone, it seems he can reach almost any level of business, government, or the communications industry. His clients include some of Canada's most intriguing enterprises and his relationship with many of them stays unknown." The writer referred to him being known as a "grey eminence" in the international business world.

In our various visits at the cottage, in Toronto or at the estate at Youngstown, NY and then in later years in his retirement in Gravenhurst, he was always Grandpa Cowan.

To be sure, the earlier generations echo in the lives of those who follow. Family traits and personalities are glimpsed in those who are children, grandchildren and beyond. A shared heritage, it continues to keep alive the people who went before us. It seems especially true as you compare grandparents to grandchildren.

The choice to invest in Muskoka when he did and to select the location he did on Mary Lake was a great legacy of family memories created and cherished for the four generations who would know the cottage.

63. Cousins by the Dozens

There was a major contrast between my two family trees. While both traced their roots in the not too distant past to Scotland, the Fairleys had my father as the only surviving child on that side with most of the other relatives still in Scotland others in British Columbia and one set in Alberta. My mother's side included three siblings with seven cousins for us in that generation. Because my Grandfather was the eldest of nine children, there were cousins by the dozens. Some of the children of his younger siblings were close in age to us. That meant large family gatherings for state occasions like weddings and funerals as well as fun picnics when some of the clan gathered.

My great-grandfather Hugh Cowan was the son of John Cowan of Oban, Scotland and Mary McLean of the Isle of Mull. Hugh was a Presbyterian minister, author and historian who served Ontario churches in Rutherford, Shakespeare, Kent Centre, Blenheim, St. Catharines, Sault Ste. Marie, Owen Sound and Manitoulin Island. He was one of the principal writers for The Algonquin Historical Society and edited the magazine "Mer Douce".

Granny Cowan was born Jean Eloise Wood. My mother's name Lois came from the middle of Eloise in her honour. Granny Cowan (as we knew her) was the matriarch of the Cowan clan. Growing up in difficult times, she spent her high school years staying with her relatives the McCrae family in Guelph, Ontario that included John McCrae who would later be renowned for his poem In Flanders Fields. Her genealogy also has been traced back to Sir Andrew Wood, Lord High Admiral of Scotland who defeated a larger and better-equipped force of English ships under Stephen Bull in a sea battle near Edinburgh in 1490.

It was special to see this kind great-grandmother of the nine Cowan offspring as a great-grandson. Our visits with her were at her home on Oakwood Ave. in Toronto not far from St. Clair Ave. We enjoyed the hustle and bustle – and the trolley buses! A popcorn vendor would be around the corner serving warm chestnuts as well as bags of steaming popcorn. It was great fun for little gaffers like us. Granny who at the time was in her 80s would play a game with us singing "Who's That Knocking At My Door" to which we would respond, "It's only me from over the sea, Barnacle Bill the Sailor." She also had a lamplighter character that we called "All's Well." We would picture him walking the streets of Scotland shouting, "Nine o'clock and all's well." On a table, she also had a very large brass fly whose wings would lift up to reveal a secret hiding place for a candy or two for good boys.

My grandfather, Jimmy Cowan was the eldest of the siblings. Here are the rest.

Aunt Jean Cowan was married to Uncle Charlie Jolliffe who was a drama teacher, television and movie actor who served in World War II in Britain and India. We would see them and their children Lonnie and Rick at Cop Bay near Tea Lake when we would visit the Fitzpatrick's cottage as the Jolliffes had a cottage further down the lake near Big Chute.

Uncle Ken Cowan was an accountant with Montreal Trust who married Frances Hollister. Uncle Ken was unusual for an accountant as he had a well-developed sense of humour with a special love of puns. He was very musical as well. Aunt Frances father was Frank S. J. Hollister who designed and created a number of the stained glass windows in Canada's Parliament Buildings and elsewhere. We enjoyed visiting with them regularly in Muskoka after they moved there to retire.

I never met Uncle Hugh Cowan who was an artist and cartoonist but who died at age 25.

Aunt Elizabeth Cowan "Aunt Betty" was a teacher in different places including Hamilton, Chatham with an exchange teaching assignment in England. While teaching in Big Chute, she and her class were the subject of David Brown Milne, the Group of Seven contemporary in the painting "Goodbye To A Teacher" which he gave her. It is now in the McMichael Gallery in Kleinberg.

Aunt Grace Cowan married John Fitzpatrick and they lived for many years in the High Park area where we would visit them. Uncle John was a champion sprinter who represented Canada in the 1928 Olympic team that included sprinter Percy Williams. He then played for the Hamilton Tiger Cats of the CFL and later served as a member of the RCMP. He was a mechanical engineer for the Province of Ontario and designed the "Fitzpatrick Domes" – those igloo-like structures that store salt and sand for winter road service. These are used in countries around the world. He also solved a problem with northern harbours freezing by creating a bubbling system that kept the ice from forming. It was installed in the Bay of Quinte at Glenora so that Highway 33 could be used year round. This allowed the ferry called the Amherst Islander to ferry cars between Glenora and the mainland. Aunt Grace was a bacteriologist at Connaught Labs – unusual for a woman of her time.

Uncle Stuart Cowan and Aunt Joan with son Hugh and daughter Nancy lived in Clarkson. They were of similar ages to us and always were fun to visit. We always marveled at the GO trains flying by and the fact that they had no telephone poles – it was all underground! Who knew that many years later we would be living just down the road in Lorne Park? Uncle Stuart was a veteran of World War II and later was a business editor and writer for the Globe & Mail.

"Uncle Don From Oregon" as the rhyme would go was one of the youngest of the nine children. Donald Cowan and his wife Diane lived in Ashland, Oregon where he was an executive with the YMCA. In addition to having four sons who were all named beginning with "D" (David, Donald, Derek & Douglas), he was the official birthday Uncle. He faithfully called each of the extended family (a huge list) on their birthday and would give them a greeting (sometimes in song) and a chat to see how they were doing. What a gift to have a connector like this in the family!

The youngest was Uncle Allan Cowan who was an economist with the Canadian government. I used to receive and read with interest his publication "Canadian Affairs" which was a monthly update of what was happening in national events. It published from 1967 to 1980.

Those many and varied family were and are valuable. It is great to be part of a larger family where you can keep in touch. Visits with members of the Fairley clan in Scotland and in Canada have also enriched our sense of who were are.

As with so many things in life like the cottage, it is only later in life that you see how important a gift they truly are.

64. To Whom Much Is Given

I have had some unwavering sources of encouragement to get this and that major project called "life" done. You probably have a list like this too. These are the people that you have met along the journey who have chosen to invest themselves into your experience. Many wonderful people make up the pages of our lives. I am grateful for each one who has taught, guided, corrected and cared for me over the book that is my life.

With the many reminiscences that are part of a personal project like this cottage book, I wanted to take the time to extend some personal thanks to some of the people who have not just been pages in my life but qualify as chapters too. So bear with me as I recount just some of these people.

To those of you with a background in reading the Bible, this may remind you a bit of the Book of Numbers. When I would read this book of "so and so begat so and so", I used to wonder why include all these names. Many of whom were otherwise unknown. But in their lifetime, they made a difference. The details are not all known to us, but they were worth mentioning. So this is my similar and incomplete attempt to recite some of the people. To others it might just be names. It would take many books to recite how and why each one is here. Suffice to say, they have made it into my "Book of Numbers."

Perhaps you will see your own list of different names who have similarly meant very much to you over the years too. In our culture, we do not pause often enough to say thank-you. Here is a small effort by me on just some of the many who have made a personal difference for me.

Generationally, I was blessed with friends of my parents who treated us like extended family and cared for me over the years: people like Maurice & Maisey Muller, Jack & Winnie Lynn, Bill & Molly Weir and Gordon & Dorothy Marsh, John & Helen Kelton, Eugene & Chris McFarlane, Dewart & Jean Lynn, John & Fern Kimmerly, Jair & Alice Hall, Harry & Pauline Carnegie and Murray & Marguerite Lynn, Margaret Spence, Mrs. Craig and Mrs. Datsun. Other people of influence in my early life were Russ & Adele Skaling, Grant & Barbara Steidl, Fred & Mary Carlson and Dr. Carl Armerding. John and Dave Lynn were our regular baby-sitters. In spite of the challenges of dealing with three very busy boys, they always had great patience.

My kindergarten Sunday School teacher was Miss Gertrude Bovey who prayed for my family and me every day. She is missed.

Ted Becker is remembered especially for his time in Gravenhurst when he would visit my then ailing Grandpa Cowan and read him Psalms and other passages from the Bible. It was comforting for him to hear those words again.

From my youth, I have had people that have been significant friends from Forest Cliff Camp days like Dave & Barbara Johnson, Dave & Helen Overholt, Art Brighton Jr., John Torrens, Dave Hill, Charlie DiMaria, Paul Charron, Lou Leissing, Paul Gowan and many more. Leaders and counsellors like Jim & Rae Sparks, Art & Jean Brighton, Charlie & Grace Mulholland, Tom & Ollie Dwinnel, Ellis Pearce, John Durley, Ross Stone, Charlie & Winnie Shorten, Harold & Greta Jackson, Rob Geottel, Steve McGinnis all played a positive part in my early experiences at camp and the life lessons learned there.

Cari's lifelong friends also shared Mary Lake experiences at their cottages Sandy Lothian Alexanian and Laurie Pratt. Another lifelong friend Debbie Marquis hosted Cari at her cottage at Wasaga Beach many times.

Dr. Norman & Ruth Ericson of Wheaton College have always been there from my first class with him through the years and over the miles. Their faithful guidance, care and prayers for us have made life so much richer. We have also enjoyed getting to know their family over the years with many happy moments with Beth & Dave Sanders and Ken & Rebecca Ericson and their families.

From my Wheaton days as a student, other students who have continued to make a difference in my life include my roommate James & his wife Beth Ernest, Dr. Bill Cook, Phil & Paulette Vosseler, Dave & Pam DeWitt, Taylor & Emily McCormick.

Also in Chicagoland are Paul & Beth Hadley, Wally & Margie Gast, Larry & Arlene Van Hook, Don & Mary Kersemeier, Al & Mary Ditthardt, Jim & Vodus Campbell along with Ray & Lola Miller. Some of my peers in those years were Beth Steidl, Doug Hadley, Wanda Grubb, Brent Felten, Cindy Carpenter, Ken Kerr, Barb Van Hook, Phil Girgis, Esther Gebhardt, Kurt Felten, Julie Gebhardt, Keith Hadley, Janet Starr, Mark Ditthardt, Evelyn Starr, Tom Van Hook and Mike Miller,. All of these knew me in my college years. They challenged my thinking and encouraged me to grow and keep growing.

Some people are a gift to you for all seasons. Murray & Barb Knights are that for us.

Gary & Wendy Carter have been foul weather friends – people who are with you in not only the good times but in the times when you are castaways adrift on a raging sea.

Later friends have been willing to share their lives with ours. Floyd & Anne McKee, Stuart & Karen Fickett, Bob & Evelyn Wilson, Jim & Erna MacNeill, George & Maureen Bell, Jim & Anna Rendle, Jack & Eudora Hannah along with Dr. Donald Loveday, Dave & Lois Black, Mike & Kathy Mawhorter. Dale & Susan Newman have been both friends and our faithful tax advisor and planner.

The Lorne Park years added many new relationships. Included here are people like: Doug & Sandy McKenzie; Dr. Bruce & Barbara Neal; Ron & Lynn McKerlie, Ward & Lois Pipher, Brian & Sharon Dymond; Ross & Beth Downing; Andras & Margaret Rameshwar; George & Kenia Alves. Others are: Clarence & Priscilla Kustra, Dale & Donna Rose, Bill & Gail Masson, Dean & Barb Dempster, Jim & Cheryl Hughes, Don & Cindy Hallman, Gordon & Nancy McKye, Ted Roberts, Drs. Ken & Janet Jansz, Julie Cuthbert, Andrea Daoust, Bruce & Laura Preston, Paul & Shauna Lee Carter. Another bonus from those years was then future son-in-law, Matt Page.

Many business friends in Toronto who have become chapters for me include: Dr. Blair & Angela Lamb, Dr. Larry & Joan Komer, Mike & Michelle Lanthier, David & Libby Garshowitz, Lisa Tata and Sandy Kapustik.

Others are Hartley & Fran Garshowitz, Aliza Garshowitz-Legge, Dr. Alvin & Carol Pettle, Lou & Marisa Rocca, John Hoey, Glenn Rogers, Justice Peter Jarvis, Justice Maurice & Heather Cullity, Bill & Catherine McVean, Marilyn Goodhand, Roy Vokes, Dr. Bryce Taylor, Joe Chuba, Norma Peckover and Jim Jones,.

The Windsor years have been tough ones for us. After two great years of being close to Mom & Dad and brother John, with grandchildren living near grandparents for the first time, we had to say a sudden goodbye to Mom as she faced an unexpected battle with cancer. That loss darkened these years here. Providing encouragement have been Banwell people including: Dr. Alex & Linda Moir, Steve & Dorothy Radin, Claude & Hyacinth Daniels, Dave & Marlee Page, Hal & Ruth Herzog, Tom & Susan Holmes and Jim Wheeler. I am thankful for Henry & Monica Nurse, Al & Grace McCann, Cheryl Martell, Ross Hickling, Joan Fulmer, Grant & Debbie Ebel, Dave Ahlstedt & Marni DeJoseph, Rod & Beth Pressey, Zelma Horvath, Elaine Dennis, Frances Dennis, Penny Bain and John Mateau. Brother Brian and his wife Carol with their daughter Morgan have recently called Windsor home again.

Windsor friends from school and business for us have included Cari's teaching partner and good friend Jenny-Lee Boyle, Bill & Paula White, Diane Bertolin, Tim & Linda Killop, Hal Sullivan, Lynnette Bain, Kim McDonald, Andrea Bondy, Sabrina Green, Dr. Kouslai Naidoo, Wayne Sauvé, Dr. Mathaven Moodley, Todd Cuthbert, Sean Sauvé, Steve Belanger, Chris & Susan Smith, Sandra Pupatello, Monica Ufholz, Pat Banks and Lauren Wells. We have also enjoyed our neighbours Mike & Jennifer Mailloux and Mike & Laura Wallace.

From the early family connections above, Winnie Lynn and Maurice Muller have had a special continuing role in our Windsor lives.

As I have said, these are only some of the many significant people who have shared in our stories. So many teachers and others will have to be listed in another book sometime!

There is nothing like old friendships that have endured. To know someone and to have been known by them from your youth gives a life perspective that is very special to experience. I am thankful for those who have endured with me.

But it is also reassuring to know that new relationships continue to be added to each of the life adventures. That's a good reason to expect great things in the years ahead.

I have been truly rich in the friendships I have known over the years and am only beginning to understand the importance of these relationships in my past and present as well as for my future.

Useful Links and Contacts

S trategic Seminars – Workshops and seminars for corporations and groups covering topics on Business, Health, Leadership, Motivation, Relationships, Team Building, Customer Service and more. We are flexible to help corporations and groups of all sizes and with different budgets. There is a special focus on leadership and group development services for corporations. Seminars  are offered in the U.S., Canada and the Caribbean. Contact us in Chicago, Detroit or Toronto. www.strategic-seminars.com

 Canadian Executive Coaching – Executive Coaching for Canadian senior executives, managers, department heads, top sales people and leaders. Serving a wide range of industry, government and not-for-profit with one on one coaching to improve performance, provide personal support and reflection. Based on a whole-person model that recognizes our different skills, passions and abilities, Canadian Executive Coaching will help you reach your full potential as a leader and as a person. Member of the Fellowship of Executive Coaches. www.canadian-executive-coaching.com

Pain physician and seminar speaker Dr. Blair Lamb, MD – Understanding and treatment of pain conditions affecting people of all ages with special focus on fibromyalgia, migraines, arthritis, whiplash and more. Extensive articles are included on different pain topics. His War On Pain video series explaining some of the

most common pain conditions and how to treat them for best results. Learn about the patented "Lamb method" of using spinal BOTOX® and other similar agents to treat low back pain and many other chronic pain conditions. www.drlamb.com

Learn about featured seminar speaker Dr. Larry Komer, MD with his innovative research and treatments using hormone therapy as part of an overall wellness and anti-aging strategy for men, women and those who have been injured. Excellent information is available on the website for women including menopause, bio-identical hormone therapies, breast cancer

and more. For men learn about andropause, testosterone, fitness and conditions affecting men. New understanding on traumatic brain injury is part of his research as well. For more information on Dr. Komer and his clinic, please visit – www.drkomer.com and www.mastersmensclinic. com

Palantir Publishing – Publisher of Grant D. Fairley's biography of television's beloved The Friendly Giant – Bob Homme. www.palantir-publishing.com

Dr. Alvin Pettle, MD is a world expert on bio-identical hormones. He is a popular speaker and writer with a practice dedicated to women's

health and wellness in Toronto, Ontario. www.drpettle. com

York Downs Pharmacy is Toronto based pharmacy with advanced compounding as well as other educational and health products and services shipping across Canada. www.yorkdownsrx.com

James A. Cowan References

Baker, Carlos (1969) Ernest Hemingway: A Life Story. New York, NY: Charles Scribner's Sons.

Burrill, William (1994) Hemingway: The Toronto Years. Toronto, ON: Doubleday Canada

Callaghan, Morley (1963) That Summer in Paris : Memories of Tangled Friendships with Hemingway, Fitzgerald and Others. New York, NY: Coward-McCann

Carroll, Jock (1981) The Life & Times of Greg Clark, Canada's Favorite Storyteller. Toronto, ON: Doubleday

Fenton, Charles A. (1958) The Apprenticeship of Ernest Hemingway - The Early Years. New York, NY: Viking Press Harkness, Ross (1963) J. E. Atkinson Of The Star. Toronto, ON: University of Toronto Press

Searle, R. Newell (1977) Saving Quetico Superior: A Land Set Apart St. Paul, MN: Minnesota Historical Press

Nolan, Michael (2001) CTV-The Network That Means Business. Edmonton, AB: The University of Alberta Press

Krishnamurthy Sriramesh (Editor), Dejan Vercic (Editor) (2009) The Global Public Relations Handbook, Revised and Expanded Edition: Theory, Research, and Practice. New York, NY: Routledge p. 655-656

Warecki, George Michael (2000) Protecting Ontario's Wilderness: A history of changing ideas and preservation politics, 1927-1973. New York, NY: Peter Lang International Academic Publishers

Knott, Leonard L (1955) The PR in Profit: A Guide to Successful Public Relations in Canada. Toronto, ON: McClelland & Stewart

Patterson, Tom and Allan Gould (1999) First Stage: The Making of the Stratford Festival. Firefly Books

Davies, Robertson and Guthrie, Tyrone (1971) Renown at Stratford Robertson and Tyrone Guthrie Toronto: Clarke, Irwin & Co.

Guthrie, Tyrone Davies, Robertson and Grant MacDonald (1954) TWICE HAVE THE TRUMPETS SOUNDED – A Record of the Stratford Shakespearean Festival in Canada

Liberty Profile: Jimmy Cowan by Ken MacTaggart, Liberty Magazine Canada April 28, 1945 Pages 16-17

Meet Cowan – Phantom of Canadian PR by Dean Walker, Marketing Magazine April 26, 1963

James A. Cowan Heads Canadian Film Institute, Canadian Film Weekly Magazine February 27, 1952 Pages 1 and 3

Various articles from The Toronto Star, Star Weekly, Esquire Magazine, The Varsity, The Goblin and Maclean's Magazine

A covering letter on White House stationary, dated April 6, 1939, written by President Franklin Roosevelt's private secretary M A LeHand to Douglas Cowan (born April 6, 1935) as a birthday greeting including a card signed by FDR. According to family members, the card followed a conversation between FDR and James Cowan where the President said, "You have been helping me out here. Besides the money we are paying, what else could I do for you?" JAC replied, "My son is having a birthday, perhaps you could send him a birthday card." The letter read, "April 6, 1939 My dear Douglas, It has come to the attention of the President that today you are celebrating your birthday and he wants to join your friends in extending congratulations and good wishes. He also asks me to send you the enclosed signed card and to express the hope that you will have a long, useful and happy life. Very sincerely yours, Signed M A LeHand Private Secretary

The Golden Gong – The Story of Rank Films (2004) DVD Hosted By Michael Caine. Kock International

Cowan Family References

John Fitzpatrick

Hawley, Samuel (2011) I JUST RAN The Life and Times of Percy Williams, World's Fastest Human. Vancouver, BC: Ronsdale Press

Elizabeth Cowan

Silcox, David P. (1996) Painting Place: The Life and Work of David B. Milne. Toronto, ON: University of Toronto Press, Scholarly Publishing Division

About the Pictures

Dedication – James A Cowan at the cottage

Acknowledgements – Emma fishing on Port Sydney Cheese Dock

Introduction – Simpler times

Into The Mist – Misty Mary Lake

The Cottage – Lois Fairley helps Grant with first steps at the cottage c. 1958

Go North Young Man – (Beginning) The "Must Stop" on the trip north

A Greater Purpose – Imagine cars from the 60s meeting on this narrow bridge

The Road More Traveled – Grant on the original cottage road

What's That Smell? – Removing the fallen tree

Warm Thoughts – Not quite central heat

Cottage Worthy – The living room at the cottage

Sounds of Silence – Harry Fairley enjoys the sunset

On The Surface – Harry Fairley crossing Mary Lake

All Creatures Great & Small – Beth and the "Chippy"

Cottage Types – Deadman's Island, Mary Lake

Clammed Up – Scott cruises the shallows

Mission Impossible – Harry Fairley and Beth

Bugged – It must be May 24 in Muskoka

The Waltons – Beth and Lois Fairley making a teddy bear

The Guest Book – Many friends and many adventures

That's Entertainment – Do not open the shed

For The Birds – Hummingbirds part of Muskoka life

Well – Well – Well – Harry Fairley & Spooky look down the 60' well

Measuring Up – Lois Fairley measures Emma

Slip Sliding Away – Dave and Helen Overholt on the Port Sydney falls

Something's Fishy – Grant with pike and friend Muffin 2.0

Don't Let The Rain Come Down! – Harry Fairley and son John

Look Up – Way Up! – Inside the boat locks on the North Branch of the Muskoka River

Many Wanderings – Misty on the cottage road

Please Pass The Salt – Grant with Algonquin deer in the 60s

Ahoy There – Doug and Beth communicate

I Know A Secret – Doug in anticipation

Not For The Faint of Heart – Doug imagines driving the Meuser boat

Ready – Set – Fire! – Cottage campfires

One Dark Night – Caught in the act again

Shaboo – Lois (Cowan) Fairley with Emma and Scott

The Man In The Green Can – Brothers Doug and Scott Fairley on the Spruce Bog Boardwalk at Algonquin Park

Take A Letter – Many stairs between beach and cottage

Courage – Doug brings down the hammer

Far and Wide and Weird – The required posed picture at the trading post

The Road Less Traveled – The Jackson family were the original cottagers in our area

Jackson Falls – Looking up to the bridge over Jackson's Falls

Half A Mile To Halvastraw – Ben and Beth Jackson c. 1964

Clean As A Whistle – Doug looks for "Clean As A Whistle"

A Fine Port – A charming village with a sense of humour

Nothing To Fear – Maybe – The Cottage Sleeps

Creative Licence – Cari Fairley painting driftwood art

About the Author

G rant D. Fairley is still the little boy who spent many days enjoying the family and fun of the cottage at Mary Lake. Remarkably, he now has four children and a son-in-law. When not in his principal roles of husband, father and friend, he enjoys a wide range of other experiences.

Grant grew up in Windsor, Ontario. He is grateful for the teachers who guided and humoured him at Glenwood, Central and Centennial schools. His enchanting university days were at Wheaton College, Wheaton, Illinois where he made wonderful friends and learned how to learn in the great tradition of a liberal arts education.

Over the years, he has had a liberal arts life with a range of activities that include teaching, writing and encouraging as common threads in the many roles. He continues to explore the faith that was passed on to him from the past generations who were faithful to pass it on to him.

Look Up – Way Up – The Friendly Giant is the biography of Robert Homme written by Grant. In addition to writing books, he is the co-author of a number of patents relating to technology and healthcare.

Most days, he is sharing with others through seminars, workshops, retreats and executive coaching. He is especially delighted to serve in his local church.

He continues to learn and grow through his relationship with his wife Cari, the children, the family and friends who are in his story. For these gifts and so much more, he is very grateful.

Grant would welcome your comments on the book and your recollections about your cottage memories. You may contact him at fairley@silverwoods-publishing.com

For more pictures, visit the website www.silverwoods-publishing.com.

Up to the Cottage

Made in the USA
Charleston, SC
03 October 2011